Catholic Bible Study

Exile and Return

(Tobit, Judith, Esther, Ezra, Nehemiah, 1 and 2 Maccabees)

by

Father Joseph L. Ponessa, S.S.D.

and

Laurie Watson Manhardt, Ph.D.

Emmaus Road Publishing
827 North Fourth Street
Steubenville, OH 43952

All rights reserved. Published in 2013
Printed in the United States of America

Library of Congress Control Number: 2013938587
ISBN: 978-1-937155-99-5

Scripture quotations are taken from the
Revised Standard Version Bible, Ignatius Second Edition (RSVCE).
The Second Catholic Edition is published by Thomas Nelson Publishing
for Ignatius Press in 2006,
with ecclesiastical approval of the
United States Conference of Catholic Bishops.

Excerpts from the English translation of the
Catechism of the Catholic Church for the United States of America
Second Edition © 1997,
United States Catholic Conference, Inc. — Libreria Editrice Vaticana.
Cited in the text as "CCC."

Cover design and layout by
Jacinta Calcut, Image Graphics & Design, www.image–gd.com

Cover artwork:
James Tissot (1836–1902), *The Flight of the Prisoners*

Nihil obstat: Reverend Jose Valliparambil, S.T.D., *Censor Deputatis*
Imprimatur: Most Reverend Michael William Warfel
Bishop of Great Falls and Billings
April 23, 2013

The *nihil obstat* and *imprimatur* are official declarations
that a book is free of doctrinal or moral error.

For additional information on the "Come and See ~ Catholic Bible Study"
series visit www.CatholicBibleStudy.net

Catholic Bible Study

Exile and Return

Introduction

"As long as they did not sin against their God they prospered,
for the God who hates iniquity is with them.
But when they departed from the way which he had appointed for them,
they were utterly defeated in many battles
and were led away captive to a foreign country;
the temple of their God was razed to the ground,
and their cities were captured by their enemies.
But now they have returned to their God,
and have come back from the places to which they were scattered,
and have occupied Jerusalem, where their sanctuary is,
and have settled in the hill country, because it was uninhabited .
Now therefore, my master and lord,
if there is any unwitting error in this people and they sin against their God
and we find out their offense, then we will go and defeat them.
But if there is no transgression in their nation, then let my lord pass them by;
for their Lord will defend them, and their God will protect them,
and we shall be put to shame before the whole world."
Judith 5:17–21

Exile and Return—Down through history, many nations have had the wrenching experience of being exiled from their ancestral homelands—Jews and Palestinians, North African Romans, Native and African Americans, Rhineland and Sudeten Germans, French Alsatians, Anatolian Armenians and Greeks, Macedonian and Bulgarian Turks, Pakistanis and Hindus, Greek Cypriots, Middle Eastern Christians, and Marsh Arabs. The litany goes on and on and seems to have accelerated in the past few centuries.

Ethnic cleansing was invented by the ancient Assyrians, and continued by the Babylonians, who physically shifted around their subject populations as a calculated strategy to destroy their sense of identity. People lost not only their patrimony in lands and property, but also the shrines associated with their ancient gods. Among the first victims of this policy were the inhabitants of Northern Israel. Eventually their southern relatives were taken away into captivity also.

Unlike too many other refugee groups, the Hebrews managed to go home again. How did they do it? One thing different about the exiled Hebrews is their concentration on sacred writings. They may have been separated from their land, temple and other institutions, but their books went with them into exile. And they continued to compose books and record their history while in exile and later. This literature gave them the sense of purpose to try to go home again. The purpose of this Bible Study is to read some of the literature that belongs to the exile and the return to Jerusalem.

Judith is written in exile. This book looks back fondly at a courageous heroine who acted on her profound faith in God to deliver His people. Judith prayed to God for strength. Then she stood up to the invaders who were about to attack her people.

Esther and Tobit are written about the exile experience itself, and how the Israelites rose to high positions of influence in their host country, while still retaining their religious and national identity and remaining faithful to the covenant.

Ezra and Nehemiah describe the Jews return from exile to Jerusalem and their efforts in rebuilding the temple, which was in ruins.

Maccabees are two books about how the people had to continue to struggle, even after returning to their own land, because of continuing pressures to abandon their values and religion. Even after returning to one's earthly home, one is not yet in heaven, our true home. We are all exiles from Paradise, and will never rest easy until we return there.

What You Need

To do this Bible Study, you will need a Catholic Bible, and the *Catechism of the Catholic Church* (CCC). The *Catechism of the Catholic Church* is available in most bookstores, and on the Internet at www.vatican.va/archive/catechism/ccc_toc.htm

In choosing a Bible, remember that the Catholic Bible contains seventy-three books. If you find Tobit in your Bible's table of contents, you have a complete Catholic Bible. The Council of Hippo approved these seventy-three books in AD 393, and this has remained the official canon of Sacred Scripture since the fourth century. The Council of Trent in AD 1546 reaffirmed these divinely inspired books as the canon of the Bible.

Archbishop Stephen Langton of Canterbury, England first introduced chapter divisions in Sacred Scripture around AD 1200. The French bookseller Robertus Stephanus first assigned verse numbers to the Bible in AD 1551. Legend has it that Stephenus did some of his work while riding in a horse drawn coach, and that the bumps in the road caused some mistakes when dividing the text into verses: his pencil jumped across the words!

For Bible study purposes, choose a word-for-word, literal translation rather than a paraphrase. Some excellent translations are the Revised Standard Version Catholic Edition (RSVCE), the Jerusalem Bible (JB), and the New American Bible (NAB). **Because of different verse numbering in these Bibles, the RSVCE second edition by Ignatius Press will be the easiest to use to complete the home study questions in the *Come and See ~ Catholic Bible Study* series.** The RSVCE Bible is available at www.EmmausRoad.org (1–800–398–5470) and on-line at www.ewtn.com/ewtn/bil for free!

How To Do This Bible Study

1. Pray to the Holy Spirit to enlighten your mind and spirit.
2. Read the commentary in this book.
3. Read the Bible passages for the first chapter.
4. Use your Bible and Catechism to write answers to the home study questions.
5. Find a small group and share your answers aloud on those questions.
6. Watch the videotape lecture that goes with this study.
7. End with a short wrap-up lecture and/or prayer.

Invite and Welcome Priests and Religious

Ask for the blessing of your pastor before you begin. Invite your pastor, associate pastor, deacon, visiting priests, and religious to participate in Bible study. Invite priests, deacons, and religious to come and pray with Bible study members, periodically answer questions from the question box, or give a wrap-up lecture. Accept whatever they can offer to the Bible study. However, don't expect or demand anything from them. Appreciate that they are very busy and don't add to them additional burdens. Accept with gratitude whatever is offered.

Practical Considerations

➤ Ask God for wisdom about whom to study with, where, and when to meet.
➤ Gather a small prayer group to pray for your Bible study and your specific needs. Pray to discern God's will in your particular situation.
➤ Show this book to your pastor and ask for his approval and direction.
➤ Choose a day of the week and time to meet.
➤ Invite neighbors and friends to a "Get Acquainted Coffee" to find out who will make a commitment to meet for ninety minutes each week for Bible study.
➤ Find an appropriate location. Start in someone's home or in the parish hall if the space is available and the pastor will allow it.
➤ Hire a babysitter for mothers with young children and share the cost amongst everyone, or find some volunteers to provide childcare.
➤ Consider a cooperative arrangement, in which women take turns caring for the children. All women, even grandmothers and women without children, should take turns, serving the children as an offering to God.

Pray that God will anoint specific people to lead your study. Faithful, practicing Catholics are needed to fill the following positions:

➤ **Teachers**—take responsibility to read commentaries and prepare a short wrap-up lecture after the small group discussion and video.
➤ **Song Leaders**—lead everyone in singing a short hymn to begin Bible study.
➤ **Prayer Leaders**—open Bible study with a short prayer.
➤ **Children's Teachers**—teach the young children who come to Bible study.
➤ **Coordinators**—communicate with parish personnel about needs for rooms, microphones, and video equipment. Make sure rooms are left in good shape.
➤ **Small Group Facilitators** will be needed for each small group. Try to enlist two mature Catholics who are good listeners to serve together as co-leaders for each small group and share the following responsibilities:

  ❖ Pray for each member of your small group every day.
  ❖ Make a nametag for each member of the group.
  ❖ Meet before the study to pray with other leaders.

❖ Discuss all the questions in the lesson each week. Begin and end on time.
❖ Make sure that each person in the group shares each week. Ask each person to read a question and have the first chance to answer it.
❖ In the discussion group, you may go around in a circle, so that each person can have a turn to read a question. After reading the question, the reader can answer the question or pass, and then others can feel free to add additional comments.
❖ Make sure that no one person dominates the discussion, including you!
❖ Keep the discussion positive and focused on the week's lesson.

❖ Speak kindly and charitably. Steer conversation away from any negative or uncharitable speech, complaining, arguing, gossip, or griping.
❖ Listen well! Keep your ears open and your eyes on the person speaking.
❖ Give your full attention to the one speaking. Be comfortable with silence. Be patient. Encourage quieter people to share first. Ask questions.
❖ If questions, misunderstandings, or disagreements arise, refer them to the question box for a teacher to research or the parish priest to answer later.
❖ Arrange for a social activity each month.

More Practical Considerations

➢ Twelve to fifteen people make the best size for small groups. When you get too many people in a group, break into two smaller groups.
➢ A group of teenagers or a young adult group could be facilitated by the parish priest, a young adult, or a young adult leader.
➢ Men share best with men and women with women. If you have a mixed Bible study, organize separate men's groups led by men and women's groups led by women. In mixed groups, some people tend to remain silent.
➢ Offer a married couples' group, if two married couples are willing to lead the group. Each person should have his or her own book.

➢ Sit next to the most talkative person in the group and across from the quietest. Use eye contact to encourage quieter people to speak up. Serve and hear from everyone.
➢ Listening in Bible study is just as important as talking. Evaluate each week. Did everyone share? Am I a good listener? Did I really hear what others shared? Was I attentive or distracted? Did I affirm others? Did I talk too much?
➢ Share the overall goal aloud with all of the members of the group. We want to hear from each person in the group, sharing aloud each time the group meets.
➢ Make sure that people share answers only on those questions on which they have written answers. Don't just share off the top of your head. Really study.

➢ Consider a nursing mothers' group in which mothers can bring their infants and hold them while sharing their home study questions.
➢ Families can work together on a family Bible study night, read the commentary and scriptures aloud and help one another to find answers in the Bible and Catechism.
➢ Parents or older siblings can read to young children and help the youngsters to do the crafts in the children's Bible study book.

Social Activities

God has created us as social creatures. Large parishes make it difficult for people to get to know one another. Some people can belong to a parish for years without getting to know others. Bible study offers an opportunity for spiritual nourishment as well as inclusion and hospitality. Occasional simple social activities are recommended in this book. In planning your social activities be a good sport and try to attend with your group.

➢ Agree on a time when most of the group can meet. This could be right before or after Bible study or a different day of the week, perhaps even Saturday morning.
➢ Invite people to come to your home for the social time. Try to offer hospitality to those God sends along your way.

> *Do not neglect to show hospitality to strangers,*
> *for thereby some have entertained angels unawares.*
> (Hebrews 13:2)

➢ Keep it simple! Just a beverage and cookies work well. Simplicity blesses others. People can squeeze together on a sofa or stand around the kitchen. Don't fuss.
➢ Help the group leader. If Bible study meets in someone's home, invite the group to come to your place for the social time. Don't make the group leader do it all.
➢ If Bible study meets at church, don't have all of the socials at church as well. Try to have some fellowship times in people's homes.

Modify times to meet your specific needs. If your parish has early morning Mass, adjust the time of your social to accommodate those members of the group who would like to attend Mass and need some time to get to the social. If lunch after Bible study makes too long of a day for children who need naps, plan the social for a different day. A mother's group might meet after school when high school students are available to baby-sit.

Class Schedule

Accept responsibility for being a good steward of time. God gives each of us twenty-four hours every day. If Bible study starts or ends late, busy people may drop out. Late starts punish the prompt and encourage tardiness. Be a good steward of time. Begin and end Bible study with prayer at the agreed upon time.

If people consistently arrive late or leave early, investigate whether you have chosen the best time for most people. You may have a conflict with the school bus schedule or the parish Mass schedule. Perhaps beginning a few minutes earlier or later could be a service to those mothers who need to pick up children from school.

Possible Bible Study Class Schedules

<u>Morning Class</u>

9:30 a.m.	Welcome, song, prayer
9:35 a.m.	Video
10:00 a.m.	Small group discussion
10:40 a.m.	Wrap-up lecture and prayer

<u>Evening Class</u>

7:30 p.m.	Welcome, song, prayer
7:35 p.m.	Video
8:00 p.m.	Small group discussion
8:40 p.m.	Wrap-up lecture and prayer

The video could be shown either before or after the small group discussion, and either before, after, or instead of a wrap-up lecture. Whether or not you choose to use the videotapes, or have a wrap-up lecture, please begin and end with prayer.

Wrap-Up Lecture

Additional information is provided in videotaped lectures, which are available for this study and can be obtained from Emmaus Road Publishing, 827 North Fourth Street, Steubenville, Ohio, 43952. You can obtain DVDs of these lectures by going to www.emmausroad.org on the Internet or by calling 1-800-398-5470. Videotaped lectures may be used in addition to, or in place of a wrap-up lecture, depending on your needs.

When offering a closing lecture, the presenter should spend extra time in prayer and study to prepare a good, sound lecture. The lecturer should consult several Catholic Bible study commentaries and prepare a cohesive, orthodox lecture. Several members of the leaders' team could take turns giving wrap-up lectures. Invite priests, deacons, religious sisters and brothers to give an occasional lecture.

The Deuterocanonical Books

Judith, Tobit and Maccabees are books that you will only find in a Catholic Bible. The Deuterocanonical Books are those books of the Old Testament that are not found in the Hebrew Bible used by the Jews in this day, but have been preserved in the Greek version of the Eastern Church and in the Latin version of the Western Church. Most Protestant Bibles omit these books, but the Council of Hippo included them in the official list for Catholic use in AD 393. The Deuterocanonica include seven whole books and two additions to other books:

> TOBIT
> JUDITH
> WISDOM
> SIRACH (Ecclesiasticus)
> BARUCH and the Letter of Jeremiah
> 1 MACCABEES
> 2 MACCABEES
> > Additions to DANIEL (Daniel 3, 13, and 14)
> > Additions to ESTHER (Esther 10:4–16:24)

The Jewish Rabbis of Jamnia in Galilee formulated the official list of books in the Hebrew canon about the year AD 90. This was sixty years after the death of Jesus, and by then the Church had already begun to use the longer list found in the Septuagint translation. Thus the Church's longer list is older than the Jewish shorter list. However, only the Jews preserved the original texts of the Old Testament books, and so the original Hebrew manuscripts of Sirach and other Deuterocanonical books were lost over time. Later discoveries have made possible nearly a complete reconstruction of the Book of Sirach, but the original language manuscripts of the other books remain unfound. Tobit may have been written in Aramaic or Hebrew. First Maccabees is found in Greek and Second Maccabees exists in Hebrew.

One value of the Deuterocanonical Books is that they cover a five hundred-year period between the Jewish Exile and the birth of Christ. Without them, there is a gap of five centuries between the Old and New Testaments. Would the Holy Spirit remain silent and not inspire any Scripture during half a millennium leading up to Jesus? Also without them, there is a major gap in the knowledge of the history of the Jewish people. So, the Deuterocanonica are associated with other "inter-testamental" writings to close these gaps, and they show the continuing development of doctrines like life after death, martyrdom, resurrection from the dead, the end of the world, and prayer for the dead. Tobit includes a version of the Golden Rule "do unto others as you would have them do unto you." The Book of Sirach recapitulates the wisdom writings of the Old Testament and sets the stage for the Sermon on the Mount. This study, *Exile and Return,* begins with the Deuterocanonical book of Tobit.

To Look Beyond

Our preaching, our proclamation, is really one-sided, in that it is largely directed toward the creation of a better world, while hardly anyone talks any more about the other, truly better world. We need to examine our conscience on this point. Of course one has to meet one's listeners half-way, one has to speak to them in terms of their own horizon. But at the same time our task is to open up this horizon, to broaden it, and to turn our gaze toward the ultimate.

These things are hard to accept for people today and seem unreal to them. Instead, they want concrete answers for now, for the tribulations of everyday life. But these answers are incomplete so long as they don't convey the sense and the interior realization that I am more than this material life, that there is a judgment, and that grace and eternity exist. By the same token, we also need to find new words and new means to enable people to break through the sound barrier of finitude.

Pope Benedict XVI Emeritus, *Light of the World*
(San Francisco, CA: Ignatius Press, 2010), 179.

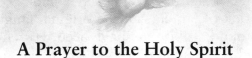

A Prayer to the Holy Spirit

O Holy Spirit, Beloved of my soul, I worship and adore You,
enlighten, guide, strengthen and console me.
Tell me what I ought to say and do, and command me to do it.
I promise to be submissive in everything You will ask of me,
and to accept all that You permit to happen to me,
only show me what is Your will.
Amen.

Chapter 1

A Good Guy
Tobit 1–3

I, Tobit, walked in the ways of truth and righteousness
all the days of my life,
and I performed many acts of charity
to my brethren and countrymen
who went with me
into the land of the Assyrians, to Nineveh.
Tobit 1:3–4

Tobit is one of the seven Deuterocanonical books, found in the Catholic Bible, but not in Protestant Bibles. There is nothing mysterious or even particularly Catholic about these books. Not included by the rabbinic Council of Jamnia, in about the year AD 90, the original Hebrew manuscripts have not been preserved. Whether they should be included in the Bible was a serious question for a long time. The Council of Hippo included these books in AD 393, and the Council of Trent in AD 1546 definitively declared that they should be included in the Catholic Bible. Hence, the Church recognizes them as inspired by the Holy Spirit.

Although the Rabbis rejected these books for inclusion in the Hebrew Bible, they recognized their fine qualities. For example, the Book of Sirach (Ecclesiasticus) is quoted more than eighty times in surviving rabbinic literature. These books are very Jewish in character, and document Jewish life and history during the last centuries leading up to the New Testament. Without these seven books, there is a gap of nearly five hundred years between the two Testaments. Would the Holy Spirit inspire nothing for five centuries immediately before the appearance of Christ? Why should there be silence? Should not that have been a time of preparation?

The Book of Tobit—Fragments of the Book of Tobit were discovered among the Dead Sea Scrolls. Some of the fragments are in Hebrew and some in Aramaic. As a result, no one knows exactly which of these two languages is the original language of Tobit. But that is not unusual. The same could be said of Ezra, Nehemiah, Daniel, First Maccabees, and even the Gospel according to Matthew. Full editions of Tobit exist in Greek, Syriac, and Latin, with significant differences between them.

As a result, it is difficult to establish the precise text of this book. The same is true of Daniel, Esther, and Jeremiah. The absence of a complete, intact, received Hebrew or Aramaic original text makes reconstruction of Tobit more problematic and very challenging. The Western Church has traditionally used the Latin text of Tobit, which was edited by Saint Jerome, while the Eastern Church has used the Greek text, which was associated with the Septuagint. Lately, however, the Western Church has begun to follow the Greek tradition more closely.

The Kingdom of Assyria During the Lifetime of Tobit

732   Ahaz of Judah appeals to Tiglath-Pileser III of Assyria for help against King Pekah of Israel. The Assyrians deport the tribes of Reuben, Gad and Manasseh to the Khabur River Valley (2 Kings 15:29).

727   (25th Tebet) King Tiglath-Pileser III dies and his son, governor Ululayu of Lebanon, comes to the throne of Assyria, taking the name Shalmaneser V.

724   Shalmeneser V raises Sargon II to co-regency and begins a siege of Samaria.

722   (12th Tebet) After taking Samaria, Shalmaneser V dies there. Sargon II, a "new man" (not of the royal dynasty), takes the throne and moves the capital of Assyria to Nineveh, and there he relocates part of the tribe of Naphtali (Tobit 1:3).

720   Sargon boasts of sending 27,290 survivors of Samaria to exile at the Khabur River. He rebuilds the city of Samaria as capital of a new province of Samerina, and settles it with Assyrian people, who intermarry with locals to become the Samaritans.

715   Hezekiah becomes king of Judea. The prophet Hosea retires (Hosea 1:1) and Isaiah and Micah prophesy for the new king.

713   Sargon II builds a new capital called *Dur-Sharrukin* "House of Sargon," and settles it with prisoners of war and deportees. Frenchmen will excavate "Khorsabad" in the 1800s and Americans in the 1930s.

711   Sargon II recaptures the rebel Philistine city of Ashdod (Isaiah 20:1), the only time his name is mentioned in the Bible.

710   Sargon II conquers Babylon and is crowned there, restoring the dual kingdom of Babylonia and Assyria.

709   (Spring Equinox in March) Sargon II leads the annual New Year procession along the Processional Way to the Temple of Ishtar in Babylon

706   Sargon II moves his court to the still unfinished city of Dur-Sharrukin.

705   Sargon II is killed in battle with the Cimmerians, is succeeded by Sennacherib, who has been in charge of the state intelligence service. He moves the capital back to Nineveh, and never mentions his predecessor again.

701   Hezekiah rebels. Sennacherib sacks Lachish (2 Kings 18:14–19:19), as shown on a bas-relief from the Palace in Nineveh. Sennacherib then besieges Jerusalem, but his forces withdraw peacefully (Assyrian sources), are slain by an angel (2 Kings 19:35), or are attacked by field mice (Herodotus).

700   Sennacherib places his son Ashur-nadir-shumi on the throne of Babylon.

694   Elamites seize Babylon and take Ashur-nadir-shumi hostage to their country.

681   Enraged by the desecration of Babylon, two of Sennacherib's sons assassinate him and flee to Egypt. He is succeeded by his youngest son, Esarhaddon, son of Queen Naqi'a, an Aramean. Tobit, about age sixty-one, is allowed to return to Nineveh (Tobit 1:22). Esarhaddon will rule until his own death in 669.

Tobit, himself, dictates the Book of Tobit in the first person. There are very few first-person writings in the Bible. Many or most of the psalmists refer to themselves in the psalms that they wrote; the author Luke breaks out into the first-person plural in parts of the Acts of the Apostles, when he was present for the events he is describing; and of course the writers of the letters of the New Testament speak in their own voice. However, the vast bulk of the Bible is told in third person. Tobit is the only entire narrative book in the Bible to be dictated by the subject himself.

The Person of Tobit—Tobit introduces himself in chapter one as an Israelite, a member of the tribe of Naphtali (from the Galilee region in the northern part of the Holy Land), who lived at the time when the Assyrians conquered the northern kingdom of Israel and carried away the people into captivity. So, Tobit spent his childhood and young adulthood in the Holy Land, but the rest of his life in captivity in Nineveh, the capital of Assyria. Tobit's name means "Good Guy" and he is the son of Tobiel, which means "God Is Good." Tobit names his son Tobias, which means "The Lord Is Good." So goodness seems to run in the family. If the main character of the story is called "Good Guy," this looks suspiciously like a parable or an allegory. However, there is so much detail to this story, of a historically accurate and biographically credible nature, that the allegory remains secondary. This is a history with a moral, but before it has a moral, it is a history.

The natural readership to whom it was especially directed had passed out of history, and so the book remained unfamiliar to Jews of other tribes. The family of Tobit, as we meet them in the Book of Tobit, are exceptional people. Tobit himself becomes procurator general, quartermaster for King Shalmaneser, and is sent on important purchasing expeditions to Media (Persia). His nephew Ahiqar becomes royal cupbearer, in effect the administrator of the entire empire. Their kinsman Gabiel in Media also has an important post there. Like Daniel and Esther, Tobit and his kinsmen rise to positions of importance in their places of exile.

Historical Struggles—In about 742 BC, a son was born to *Tobiel* of the northern tribe of Naphtali. On the eighth day after his birth, this son was circumcised and named *Tobit* "Good Guy." After his father's death, Tobit was taken into the home of his grandmother Deborah, a woman of great generosity. More than sixty years later, Tobit would pay tribute to her memory in a brief autobiography, which forms the first part of the book of Tobit (Tobit 1:1–3:6). Told in the first person, this text connects the author's life with the tumultuous events through which he lived.

When Tobit was about ten years old in 732 BC, the full force of Assyrian fury fell upon the northern kingdom of Israel. King Tiglath-Pileser II, in keeping with his policy of translocating populations, deported the tribes of Reuben, Gad and Manasseh to the Khabur River in upper Mesopotamia (2 Kings 15:29). The tribe of Naphtali seems to have been initially spared, and so Tobit continued to live for a few more years on tithes and personal gifts. When Tobit was fifteen years of age, the King of Assyria died and was succeeded by Ululayu, taking the name Shalmaneser V. The new king captured the northern capital of Samaria after a three-year siege, and died soon thereafter.

When Tobit was about twenty years old in 722 BC, a usurper claimed the throne of Assyria, taking the name Sargon II. Among his first acts was the exile of the 27,290 surviving inhabitants of the city of Samaria to the Khabur region. He relocated the tribe of Naphtali to soft exile in the cities of his empire—Tobit went to the new Assyrian capital of Nineveh, his kinsmen Gabael and Raguel to the Median cities of Rages and Ecbatana. The Naphtalites thrived in their new homes. Tobit was given the position of quartermaster for the royal court, and eventually his nephew Ahiqar was made royal cupbearer, the second position in the realm. After seventeen years of rule, Sargon II died, and his memory was banned by his successor. The name Sargon appears only in his own inscriptions, not those of his successors, or in any biblical passage, except once in Isaiah. The Book of Tobit follows this law by calling Sargon by the name of his short-lived predecessor, Shalmaneser. Far from being ahistorical, this follows the pattern of literary composition in that time period.

Approaching his fortieth birthday, after spending half his life in exile, things started going badly for Tobit and his people. The new king Sennacherib was not very secure in his first years. Vassal kings, including Hezekiah of Judah tested him. Sennacherib led an expeditionary force, capturing many of the daughters of Zion, the smaller cities of the kingdom of Judah, and even successfully besieging the fortress city of Lachish. Later he decorates the Palace in Nineveh with a bas-relief, now in the British Museum, portraying the sack of Lachish and the carrying away of Judeans into captivity. Sennacherib then besieged Jerusalem, but his army was devastated by an angel (2 Kings 19:35) or an attack of field mice, according to Herodotus. Sennacherib's own inscriptions describe this as a great victory, but Tobit reports that in his rage he carried out a pogrom in Nineveh against the Jews—probably the most recent captives, not those already assimilated into Assyrian society. Tobit then gets himself into serious trouble by burying the dead, as he had done before, and is forced to flee Nineveh. His property is confiscated, though his family members are spared.

When Tobit is sixty years of age, Sennacherib is assassinated by two of his sons, and his youngest son Esarhaddon takes the throne. Esarhaddon, son of Sennacherib's second wife, Queen Naqi'a, an Aramaean, has more sympathy for the Semitic elements of his population. He reappoints Tobit's nephew Ahiqar as royal cupbearer, and Ahiqar manages to bring Tobit back from exile and restore him to his home and family. From now on, Tobit will struggle with spiritual forces rather than historical ones. At the beginning of chapter two, the tenor of the book changes.

Spiritual Struggles—Tobit's troubles are related to his attempts to continue practicing the religion of his homeland although now he finds himself in exile. It is never easy to keep customs alive in a foreign land. The plants and animals are strange, the terrain is alien, the very air breathes differently. The neighbors have unusual customs, and it is so easy to get into trouble without knowing why. Social isolation can result in depresssion and mental illness. Tobit feels what his fellow refugees and displaced persons have felt in every time and place.

Tobit gets into trouble for burying his dead kinsmen, who have been left on the countryside by the Assyrians, reflecting different customs of disposing of the dead. The Hebrews followed a simplified Egyptian practice of embalming and burial. The Egyptians mummified, while the Hebrews simply washed the body and wrapped it in burial spices, but in both cases high respect was paid for the body of a deceased person. The Assyrians, on the other hand, had a practice shared with the Persians and some Native Americans, of exposing the corpse on a platform, to be consumed by the birds of the air. In their theology, the birds conveyed the deceased to heaven, to the high god Ahura Mazda. The Assyrians loathed burial, while the Hebrews abhorred exposure to the carrion birds. Two very different cultures and religions meet in the Book of Tobit, and fail to understand each other.

There actually are three main ways that cultures have dealt with death:

1) Egyptians, Jews, and Christians bury their dead. Burials have been found going back many thousands of years, well before the beginnings of civilization. Burial seems to have been connected with belief in an after-life even in the prehistoric period. Remains of flower bouquets have been found on early burials, and while we could not have understood what those early people were saying in their funeral rituals, the flowers are a powerful symbol, meaning exactly the same thing then that they mean today—life.

2) Assyrians, Persians and Native Americans expose their dead to the carrion birds. This too could have been an act of faith in an after-life, in the sky, conceived in a graphic, material way.

3) Hindus, Greeks, Romans, and Vikings burn their dead. For the Hindus, this practice links to their doctrine of reincarnation. For other peoples the practice seems to have indicated a "nothingness" at the end of earthly life. Cremation has been allowed among Christians—as for example in time of plague—but only if it does not mean a denial of afterlife. The doctrines of the Last Day and of the General Resurrection of the Dead must be clearly expressed.

Tobit regards the burial of a dead kinsman as so important that he makes himself ritually impure on the Feast of Pentecost doing so. This book is an important source for knowledge of Hebrew customs in the celebration of Pentecost. Whereas Passover had a ritual evening meal with lamb, it seems that Pentecost had a ritual breakfast with fish. One translation of Tobit 2:2 indicates small fishes on the menu that morning. Later in the book, the fish will continue to play an important supportive role in the narrative. Similarly, in the New Testament, the catching of fish, and the multiplication of loaves and fishes is a recurring Pentecost theme.

The birds which are deprived of their lunch that Pentecost Day retaliate in the evening by bombing Tobit with their droppings, depriving him of his sight. Tobit is in an elemental struggle now, allied with the fish against the birds. The birds seem to represent the winged gods of the Assyrians, while the fish retain a more pure relationship with their Creator. Commentators see these as reflections of primitive medical practices, where fish parts are prized for their healing properties.

Opposed by the forces of history, then by acts of nature, spurned by his neighbors, Tobit faces the unkindest cut of all—scorn from his wife. Just as the unnamed wife of Job told him to put himself out of his misery and die, so Anna, the wife of Tobit, rebukes him. In Tobit's case, he deserves the scolding. He did not accuse his wife of stealing the goat, but of unknowingly receiving stolen property. Tobit fears that the goat is a set-up, to get his family in trouble with the law again. Anna, however, in her frustration, speaks as if she might have been one of Job's so-called friends. Then Tobit's first-person narrative concludes with his appeal for death in chapter three.

After Tobit 3:7, the narrative changes to the third person, and a whole new scenario opens up—a new location, new characters, and a new problem. The young woman Sarah is also in a spiritual struggle. She has buried seven young husbands, practically wiping out a whole generation of male relatives. All this is caused by an evil demon, *Asmodeus*, a Greek version of the Persian term *aeshma daeva*, meaning "demon of wrath." The demon loves Sarah and will not share her with a human husband. Sarah has a problem and so do her wealthy parents. She is their only child. They can offer a large dowry, their entire estate. Word undoubtedly has spread, however, to relatives of every degree that marriage to Sarah means instant death.

Naturally, the eligible bachelors flee as far away as possible. As a result, Sarah's prospects of living a long life in shame, and dying unmarried are great. Sarah's prayer for death is less demanding than that of Tobit, however. Sarah does not say, as Tobit does, that it would be better to die. Instead she asks God, if he is pleased not to slay her, to look upon her favorably and have pity on her and remove her reproach. Sarah's prayer has a better ending than Tobit's, but both prayers begin with absolute praise of God, and as a result both prayers are pleasing to God on high.

---

1. From which tribe of Israel did Tobit come? Tobit 1:1

2. What kind of a man was Tobit? Tobit 1:3

* Describe a "Good Guy" who comes to your mind.

3. What can you learn about Tobit from these passages?

Exodus 23:14
Deuteronomy 16:16–17
Tobit 1:6–7

4. To whom did Tobit give his third tithe? Why? Tobit 1:8

5. Describe the events in Tobit 1:9.

6. Where did Tobit move? Why? Tobit 1:10–15

7. What corporal works of mercy did Tobit perform? Tobit 1:16–18

* What works of mercy do you regularly perform?

8. What are the spiritual and corporal works of mercy? CCC 2447

Spiritual	Corporal

* Circle the ones above that you could do this coming week.

9. How does the Christian community say farewell to the dead? CCC 1690

10. How does the Catholic Church show respect for the dead?

CCC 2299	
CCC 2300	

CCC 2301

11. What condition does the Church place on cremation? CCC 2301

12. What happened to Tobit next? Tobit 1:19–20

13. Describe the relationship between Ahikar and Tobit. Tobit 1:21–22

14. What did Ahikar do for Tobit? Tobit 1:22

15. How does Tobit respond to abundance? Tobit 2:1–2

* How do you respond when you have more than you need?

16. Describe the drama in Tobit 2:3–10.

17. Explain the argument between Tobit and Anna. Tobit 2:11–14

* Do you find it hard to accept kindness or charity from others? Explain.

18. In your own words, explain Tobit's prayer. Tobit 3:1–6

19. Explain Sarah's plight and her prayer. Tobit 3:7–15

20. How are their prayers answered? Tobit 3:16–17

Chapter 2

A Good Family
Tobit 4–9

"Blessed are you, O God of our fathers,
and blessed be your holy and glorious name for ever.
Let the heavens and all your creatures bless you.
You made Adam and gave him Eve his wife
as a helper and support.
From them the race of mankind has sprung.
You said, 'It is not good that the man should be alone;
let us make a helper for him like himself.'
And now, O Lord, I am not taking this sister of mine because of lust,
but with sincerity.
Grant that I may find mercy and may grow old together with her."
Tobit 8:5–7

The family members of Tobit—include exceptional people. Tobit himself becomes procurator general, quartermaster for King Shalmaneser (Sargon) and is sent on important purchasing expeditions to Media (Persia). His nephew Ahikar becomes a royal cupbearer, in effect the administrator of the entire empire. Their kinsman Gabael in Media also has an important post there. Like Daniel and Esther, Tobit and his kinsmen rise to positions of importance in their place of exile.

Having lost land and property, temple and government, the Hebrew tribes still had their family units to provide them with social coherence. The family is the building block of a nation. A family can exist without a country, but a country cannot exist without families. The modern ingressions on family life are actually far more socially disturbing than the exiling of an entire nation with families intact. The interaction of all the members of Tobit's family illustrate with clarity the continuity of customs preserved within the Hebrew home in exile.

Tobit provides the names of his father, his grandfather, his great-grandfather and his great-great-grandfather. Very few of us today could do this. Surnames did not exist in those days, and so you identified your father in order to show in which family you belonged. It was also important among ancient authors, to list their ancestors as part of establishing their authenticity. Many books of the Old Testament, and even some in the New Testament, contain genealogies. Lists of ancestors abound in Genesis, Numbers, Deuteronomy, Ruth and elsewhere. The farther back your named ancestors went, the more likely one of your readers would discover having a shared ancestor with you. That would establish a bond of kinship between author and reader. Any member of the tribe of Naphtali would have felt especially connected to the Book of Tobit. The fact that the tribe of Naphthali has disappeared from history, as one of the "lost tribes," can help explain why the Book of Tobit did not make the final cut into the Hebrew Bible.

Prominent women appear in Tobias' family tree—grandmother Deborah raised Tobit, mother Anna, bride Sarah, mother-in-law Edna. Rather than the patriarchal genealogy that dominates regal lineage, for ordinary people, the role of the woman is prominent. Kings had multiple wives. Regular Hebrews, like Moses and Tobit, had one wife. Monogamy, God's original design, was the norm for many generations. Jews inherit tribal affiliation from the mother. Tobit's father may have been a Naphtalite, but Tobias belongs to that tribe because of his mother Anna. Her name is spelled Anna because the book of Tobit was preserved in Greek and Latin—and Latin has no aspirant "h" consonant. That is how Hallelujah became Alleluia. The Hebrew original of the woman's name, to which she herself answered, was Hannah. The same is true of Anna of the tribe of Asher, the prophetess who greets the infant Jesus in the temple (Luke 2:36), as well as of Saint Anne, the mother of the Blessed Virgin Mary. All of these later women were named after one of the truly great woman of the Hebrew Bible, Hannah the mother of the prophet Samuel (1 Samuel 1:2–2:21). The name Hannah or Anna means "grace" in Hebrew, and all of these were women of grace.

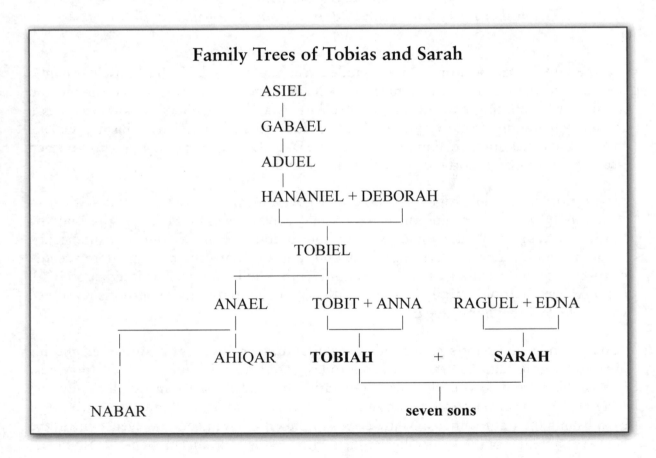

Family Trees of Tobias and Sarah

ASIEL
|
GABAEL
|
ADUEL
|
HANANIEL + DEBORAH
|
TOBIEL
|
ANAEL   TOBIT + ANNA   RAGUEL + EDNA
|
AHIQAR   **TOBIAH**   +   **SARAH**
|
NABAR   **seven sons**

The family of Tobit was geographically scattered into two different countries, some at Nineveh in Assyria and some at Ecbatan and Rages in Media (Persia). This is a blessing because they could provide places of refuge to each other in time of trouble. But, it is also a grief, because they are unable to share holydays and ordinary days with each other, or to see each other for many, many years. In those days, before text messaging and video-phones, before even snail mail or electronic mail, before telephone or telegraph, even short distances of a hundred miles or less would have meant a chasm. The excellent road system of the Persians and Romans was still many centuries in the future. The only way to communicate with faraway relatives was to send a member of the family with letters and heirlooms, over desert tracks and waterways, beset by danger from hostile beasts and thieves. Many a family member set out on an important journey, never to be seen again, and his satchel of letters fell into disreputable hands.

Roads to Media seem to have become passable again under King Esarhaddon, after years of instability under Sennacherib. Still, Anna fears for her son Tobias to undertake the journey to see relatives in Media. Only because they desperately need their money, which had been deposited with relatives, is she ultimately willing to let him go. Tobias may be a mother's boy, which seems entirely natural under the circumstances. She has only one child, who will be her sole support when she can no longer work herself. Tobias is probably already older than his father was when he was taken away to Assyria as an exile, but Tobit had a brother Anael, and the two of them had to be self-reliant because their father had died when they were boys. Tobit would have been willing to make the trip to Media himself, as he had already done many times, but his blindness would not have allowed his safe travel.

Meet the archangel Raphael—The term archangel appears only twice in the Bible (1 Thessalonians 4:16; Jude 9). Christian tradition assigns the rank of archangel to four named angels: Michael, Gabriel, Raphael, and Uriel. Michael appears to Daniel (Daniel 10:13–21; 12:1) and is described as battling Satan (Jude 9; Revelation 12:7). Gabriel appears to Daniel (Daniel 8:16; 9:21), to Zechariah (Luke 1:19), and to the Blessed Virgin Mary (Luke 1:26). Raphael appears only here in the Book of Tobit, but becomes more accessible for a longer period of time than any of the other archangels. Uriel appears in the Jewish sources Esdras IV and Testament of Solomon, as well as in the patristic writings of Pseudo-Dionysius and Gregory the Great, and is depicted as the angel who destroyed the hosts of Sennacherib before the gates of Jerusalem.

Raphael means "God heals," and his function in the Book of Tobit aligns closely with this etymology. However, Raphael has a more complex role to play in the book—traveling companion, marriage counselor, and friend. While interacting with the family of Tobit, Raphael uses a nom de guerre of Azariah, a very common Hebrew name. No fewer than twenty-eight men in the Hebrew Bible bear this name, including one who would later appear as one of the three young men in the fiery furnace in the Book of Daniel. The reluctance of Raphael to reveal his true name bears resemblance to the reluctance of God to make His proper name known to Moses. Names have a certain mystical power. Knowledge of someone's name gives the ability to bless or curse in that name. Raphael moves about in human society under a pseudonym in order to retain total control over the situation. He probably did not mind so much whether Tobias knew his name, but he certainly did not want the demon to learn it.

The Archangel Raphael fulfills a function of the journey as if he were a guardian angel for Tobias. Of course, Tobias has his own proper guardian angel, who had watched over him from the time of his conception. However, because of the extraordinarily difficult circumstances, which Tobias would have to face, and in answer to the prayers of Tobit and Sarah, God sends an archangel to reinforce the guardian angel Tobias already had. In fact, then, Tobias is accompanied on his journey by two angels, his guardian angel and the Archangel Raphael.

Choirs of Angels

Seraphim, Cherubim, Thrones
Dominions, Virtues, Powers
Principalities, Archangels, Angels

According to Pseudo-Dionysius the Areopagite, there are nine choirs of angles, subdivided into three spheres. The highest sphere is Seraphim, Cherubim, and Thrones. The middle domain contains Dominions, Virtues, and Powers. The lower sphere holds Principalities, Archangels, and Angels. Tobias travels in company with representatives from the lower angelic ranks. The higher ranks were busy adoring God in heaven, keeping the world turning, or supervising nations.

Mode of transportation—In art, Tobias always appears traveling on foot. There is no mention of any riding animal or pack animal in the biblical account. Four means of transportation were available in the ancient world:

> ➤ Camel was first-class travel for the very wealthy and royalty. Only the camel could cross the deep desert, and could take shortcuts off the normal caravan routes. Camels were twice as fast as any other means of transportation.
> ➤ Horse was good travel for those of some means. Saint Paul was supplied with a horse for his mission to Damascus to arrest Christians, because in one account Christ accuses him of over-using the stirrups to goad his animal.
> ➤ Donkey was useful both for transporting small loads and for conveying women and small children. Artists usually show Joseph walking ahead and leading Mary aback a donkey to Bethlehem. Zachariah prophesied that the Messiah would enter Jerusalem seated upon a donkey, the foal of a donkey. Tobias apparently could not afford a camel, a horse, or even a donkey.
> ➤ Foot—Only the poorest of the poor, and only the most physically fit of the poor, would have set out to travel all the way from Nineveh to Ecbatan on foot. In Renaissance art everything looks very picturesque with Raphael, Tobias, and his dog journeying by foot. That method of transportation was not for the faint-hearted, however, or for the weak-kneed, or the unfit.

The return journey, however, is different. There are male and female slaves, oxen, sheep, asses, and camels—yes, camels! Tobias upgrades from steerage class on the outbound journey to first class on his way home.

The Marriage—Different cultures contract marriage differently. In Catholic theology, the Sacrament of Matrimony is entered into by the free choice and exchange of consent between an eligible man of sufficient maturity and an eligible woman of sufficient maturity, in the presence of God and the Church's witnesses. In ancient cultures, marriage was often seen as an alliance between two families, and the legal contract of marriage was established by an agreement between the heads of the families. The Book of Tobit reflects that thinking. Since in this case, one of the two fathers-in-law is unavailable for the signing ceremony, the groom and the bride's father affix their seals to the contract. One imagines that the bride and her mother are involved behind the scenes as well.

Love emerges even in contractual marriages, for love is a decision more than merely an emotion. When Tobias learns from the angel that God has chosen Sarah for him, he falls in love with her, without ever having seen her. This shows his faith in God, the author of marital happiness. Note the psychological and spiritual truths demonstrated here. One can fall in love with things unseen. The greatest commandment is to love God, whom none of us on earth have ever seen. Love desires sight, but love does not require sight. The yearning of love is contained in being emotionally attached to what we do not actually yet possess. In a relationship of love there is always yearning, because even the shortest absence can make the heart grow fonder, and yet even in the presence of the loved one something of the invisible essence of the person remains unattained by the other. Tobias' greatness of heart did not lay in loving Sarah before he met her, but in truly loving her despite the danger.

In this case, Edna weeps for the wedding of her only child, just as she has already wept seven times before. In this case, she genuinely loves Tobias and wishes him well. She weeps for him, anticipating his death, and for Sarah, anticipating her shame. Even if the marriage turns out miraculously to succeed, she is still losing her only child. So, her weeping has many facets. While she weeps, her husband goes out to dig their new son-in-law's grave. He probably weeps too.

The happy marriage of Tobias and Sarah has become a paradigm more powerful even than the marriage of Adam and Eve. Our first parents enjoyed the gift of a successful marriage, their only privilege that was not lost in the fall. Their relationship became a conspiracy against God, however, and the whole human race became heirs to the dysfunction of their relationship. Tobias and Sarah, by getting down on their knees and praying together on their wedding night, create a more powerful matrimony, liberated from anything sinful, basking in the grace of God. Their wedding ceremony lasts so long that Archangel Raphael is able to bring back the relatives from Rages to join the wedding party—by camel, no doubt.

The Exorcism—The burning of the fish liver and gall bladder is not a voodoo ritual designed to gain mastery over occult forces. Fortunately, this practice has not become part of the standard marriage ritual, because the smell must have been ghastly. The burning did not occur in isolation, but in tandem with prayer. The prayer was the critical ingredient in the ritual of exorcism, then as now. The demon flees to Upper Egypt because that was his original homeland. This particular demon had been afflicting the Hebrews for hundreds of years, and now the definitive exorcism sends him back and binds him in the burning desert. While a full-scale exorcism may not be required in the vast majority of weddings, the resort to the Sacrament of Confession, the use of holy water, the blessing of the rings, and the reception of Holy Communion all work to expel any influence of the devil in the marriage. When both of the partners have been baptized, they have each been exorcized already in the rite of Baptism.

Sarah had the good example of her parents' Raguel and Edna's happy marriage. Through no fault of her own, she knew the grief of widowhood seven times before she could ever achieve the goal that never left her consciousness. Tobias had the good example of his parents' Tobit and Anna's happy marriage, though it was stressed at the moment due to the circumstances of his father's blindness and financial woes. Tobias, too, knew the goal he had of a strong marriage. Sarah and Tobias had a shared goal, which formed the basis of a happy life together thereafter. They both wanted what God wanted, and in that way they could not go wrong.

---

1. Identify the source of instruction that Tobit gives Tobias.

Exodus 20:12
Sirach 7:27–28
Tobit 4:1–5
CCC 2215
CCC 2216–2217

"Archangel Raphael with Tobias"

Andrea del Sarto (1486-1530)

* List some ways in which to improve the honor given to parents.

2. Find some common wisdom in these passages.

Tobit 4:4–6	
John 3:21	
James 3:13–18	

3. What practice is encouraged in Tobit 4:7–11?

4. What can you learn about the importance of the family to society?

Tobit 4:12–13	
CCC 2204	
CCC 2205	
CCC 2206	
CCC 2207	

5. To whom should one go for counsel? Tobit 4:18

* Who would you seek out for counsel if you had a need?

6. Why is Tobit sending Tobias to Media? Tobit 4:19–5:3

7. Describe the drama in Tobit 5:1–16.

8. How does Anna feel about this journey? Tobit 5:17–22

9. Describe the drama in Tobit 6:1–8.

10. Describe Sarah's troubles. Are evil spirits real? How do you get rid of them?

Tobit 3:7–8; 6:9–17
CCC 391, 395
CCC 1237
CCC 1673

* What would you say to someone who doesn't believe in the devil or evil spirits?

11. How did Raguel and Edna receive Tobias? Tobit 7:1–9

** How do you receive unexpected visitors in your home?

12. Describe the drama in Tobit 7:9–15.

13. What did Edna do? Tobit 7:16–18

14. How did Tobias deal with the demon? Tobit 8:1–3

15. When the bridal couple were alone, what happened? Tobit 8:4

16. Outline the major points of Tobias' Wedding Prayer.

Tobit 8:5	
Tobit 8:6	
Tobit 8:7	

* Describe the strongest marriage you have ever seen.

17. Where does the Sacrament of Matrimony originate? CCC 1603–1605

* Whose idea was marriage? What risks does redefining marriage bring?

18. Outline Raguel's Prayer.

Tobit 8:15	
Tobit 8:16	
Tobit 8:17	

19. Describe the wedding feast. Tobit 8:19–21

20. What happened in Tobit 9?

** Who benefits from strong marriages? Who suffers from broken marriages?

Chapter 3

The Good Tribe
Tobit 10–12

*"Praise God and give thanks to him; exalt him and give thanks to him
in the presence of all the living for what he has done for you."*
Tobit 12:6

Tobit belonged to the tribe of Naphtali. Histories of the twelve tribes of Israel line the shelves of libraries, but very few full-length studies have appeared of individual tribes, apart from Judah and Levi. Knowledge of the other tribes is scanty and fragmentary, providing insufficient data for the construction of a well-rounded sense of their history. In the case of the tribe of Naphtali, however, the Book of Tobit provides an ancient mirror into the customs and character of a tribe in exile—how they celebrated feasts, buried the dead, procured spouses, celebrated matrimony, and preserved their identity.

Naphtali in the Land of Canaan—Dan and Naphtali were the two sons of Bilhah, the handmaiden of Jacob's wife, Rachel. The sons of concubines were subordinate to the sons of wives; thus Naphtali was a follower among his brothers, not a leader. When Rachel, unlike her fertile sister Leah, was unable at first to conceive, she gave her maidservant Bilhah to Jacob in her place (Genesis 30:4). The first issue of this union was Dan, and the second was Naphtali. When Naphtali was born, Rachel said, *"With mighty wrestlings I have wrestled with my sister, and have prevailed"* (Genesis 30:8), and the author of Genesis says that it was Rachel, not Bilhah, who gave Naphtali his name, which means "wrestling."

Rachel initially embraced the children of her servant Bilhah, though they were not her blood kin, over her nephews, the children of her sister Leah. When Rachel finally had children of her own, however, she transferred her love from Dan and Naphtali to her own sons Joseph and Benjamin. Naturally, Dan and Naphtali were deeply wounded by the loss of Rachel's love, and the result was jealousy toward their half-brothers. Jacob favored Joseph over all his sons, but Dan and Naphtali had a special reason for bad feelings, having also lost the motherly love of Rachel when Joseph was born. When Joseph was seventeen, and shepherding flocks with the sons of Bilhah and Zilpah, he gave an ill report of them to their father (Genesis 37:2). The nature of the report remains unclear, but it seems that the half-brothers learned of Joseph's bad account to their father, which elevated the feelings of envy into outright hostility, taken to fever pitch by the two dreams of Joseph (Genesis 37:5–11). Still, it was not the sons of Bilhah and Zilpah who first proposed the death of Joseph, but Judah, son of Leah. The sons of concubines were subordinate to the sons of wives, subordinate in shepherding, and subordinate in conspiracy too. Each had a vote, but Naphtali was a follower in the family, not a leader.

Naphtali in Egypt—All of Jacob's sons, except Benjamin, went down to Egypt to procure grain in the time of famine, and there they found Joseph, the brother whom they had betrayed, in charge of the country. After they recognized him, on their second trip, Joseph invited the whole family to settle in Egypt. Naphtali married and fathered four sons—Jahzeel, Guni, Jezer and Shillem (Genesis 46:24). On his deathbed, Jacob gave a special blessing to each of his sons. Jacob said, *"Naphtali is a deer let loose, that bears comely fawns"* (Genesis 49:21). Apparently, Jacob approved of the grandchildren from Naphtali. From this time onwards, the heraldic image of the tribe of Naphtali would be a running deer.

Naphtali in the Desert—At the time of the census in the desert, Moses chose one man to count for each tribe. The leader for the tribe of Naphtali was Ahira, the son of Enan (Numbers 1:15). The tabulation for the Naphtalites was 53,400 able men (Numbers 1:43). The tribe lost men in the desert, due to plague and famine. Naphtali was reduced to 45,400 (Numbers 26:50). When Moses finished setting up the tabernacle in the desert, the twelve tribes brought offerings to the Lord. Ahira, son of Enan, brought the offering for Naphtali on the twelfth day (Numbers 7:78–83). Naphtali was the last of the twelve tribes, bringing up the rear liturgically, but also in the march (Numbers 10:27–28). When Moses was nearing death, he blessed the twelve tribes of Israel. *"O Naphtali, satisfied with favor, and full of the blessing of the LORD, possess the lake and the south"* (Deuteronomy 33:23), referring to the portion of the Holy Land that the tribe of Naphtali would occupy. Moses designated six tribes to stand on Mount Gerizim pronouncing the blessings, and the other six tribes to stand on Mount Ebal pronouncing the curses. Naphtali was part of the latter group (Deuteronomy 27:13).

Naphtali in the Holy Land—Moses appointed a leader for each tribe to divide the inheritance of the land. Naphtali's leader was Pedahel, son of Ammihud (Numbers 34:28–29). Naphtali's portion was in Lower Galilee, encompassing nineteen cities with their villages (Joshua 19:32–39). Walls enclosed sixteen of these cities—Ziddim, Zer, Hamath, Rakkath, Chinereth, Adamah, Ramah, Hazor, Edrei, Enhazor, Yiron, Migdalel, Horem, Beth-anath, Beth-shemesh, and Kedesh, which was set apart as one of the six sanctuary cities (Joshua 20:7). The Naphtalites allowed the Canaanites of Beth-anath and Beth-shemesh to continue living in those two cities (Judges 1:33). Three cities of Naphtali—Kedesh, Hammothdor, and Kartan—were given to the Levites of Gerson's clan to inhabit.

One of the early judges of Israel was Barak the son of Abinoam from Kedesh in Naphtali (Judges 4:6). As a result, Naphtali is credited with producing one of the great judges. But, his hometown of Kedesh was inhabited by Levites of the clan of Gerson, so perhaps Barak was a Levite. In any event, he did summon Naphtalite warriors to fight against Sisera and Jabin (Judges 4:10). The song of Deborah and Barak pays tribute to them: *"Zebulun is a people that jeoparded their lives to the death; Naphtali too, on the heights of the field"* (Judges 5:18).

When the Israelites went to Hebron to elect David as king over all twelve tribes, the Naphtalites had one thousand commanders with thirty-seven thousand armed men (1 Chronicles 12:34). The Naphtalies brought fig cakes, raisin clusters, wine, and oil on camels, mules, oxen, and sheep for the three-day celebration when David accepted the throne (1 Chronicles 12:40). During David's reign, each tribe served the king in divisions. Chief officer for the Naphtalites was Jeremoth, son of Azriel (1 Chronicles 27:19). King Solomon engaged a man of mixed blood, Hiram of Tyre, as chief builder of the temple in Jerusalem (1 Kings 7:14). Hiram (the same name as the reigning king of Tyre) was the son of a Phoenician man and a Napthalite widow. Another Naphtalite, Ahimaz, had enough prominence to claim Basemath, daughter of Solomon, for his wife (1 Kings 15:20). King Asa of Jerusalem later bribed King Benhadad of Damascus to attack the northern kingdom of Israel, and Benhadad conquered all the land of Naphtali.

Naphtali in Assyria—Tiglath-Pileser III captured all the land of Naphtali in 732 BC and carried the people captive to Assyria (2 Kings 15:29). However, later deportations took place in stages, with the royalty carried away first, then the elites, and finally the common people. The deportation of the Naphtalites probably took place over the course of a decade, beginning under Tiglath-Pileser, continuing under Shalmaneser V, and concluding under Sargon II. Tobit, son of Tobiel, was not royal, but being fairly well-to-do seems to have been deported in the second or third wave to Nineveh, which became the capital of Assyria at the beginning of the reign of Sargon II in 722 BC.

The land of Naphtali did not sit fallow for long. The agricultural capability made it too important to be abandoned altogether. The Canaanites who inhabited the cities of Beth-anath and Beth-shemesh in Naphtali remained. The Levites in Kedesh, Hammon and Kiriathaim (1 Chronicles 6:76) were taken away to Assyria, functioning as priests for the Naphtalites in exile, but other Levites likely came to these cities from the south, to maintain their claim upon them. By the time of King Josiah, the territory of the kingdom of Judah extended all the way north into the portion of Naphtali. That pious king Josiah demolished the pagan altars in his realm, even in ruined cities as far as Naphtali (2 Chronicles 34:6–7).

Some Naphtalites thrived in captivity in Assyria. Tobit held a position of great importance, as quartermaster for the royal palace. His nephew Ahiqar rose even higher, becoming cupbearer and second in command to the king himself. The kinsmen of Tobit in Media prospered, traveling from place to place on camels. Only the very wealthy could afford transportation by camel. So, within fifty years of leaving their prosperous corner of the Holy Land, the Naphtalite exiles were riding camels from Nineveh to Ecbatan to Rages. They were exiles living in high style.

The Naphtalites never forgot that they were no longer living in their own country. King Sennacherib reminded them of their plight when, after he failed to capture Jerusalem in 701 BC, he conducted a pogrom of Jews in Nineveh. The Book of Tobit is the only source that recounts this experience of persecution. Even if the Naphtalites themselves were not the object of the attacks, they would have suffered in seeing fellow Israelites of other tribes being slaughtered and left for dead in the streets. One may do well in exile, without ever being able to have the sense of security that comes from living safely and securely in one's own country.

Napthali in Persia—King Sargon II of Assyria sent some Naphtalite deportees onwards into Media (Persia), to be settled in the cities of Ecbatana and Rages. Persian rule was less harsh than Assyrian rule, so these Naphtalites had a better time of it. The Persians ended up destroying Assyria, and later Babylon as well, and so the Israelites who lived in Persia were able to enjoy the fruits of victory, in addition to providing hospitality for kinsmen from those conquered lands.

The Hebrews in Persia spread eastward into India, west to the Fertile Crescent, and north to Turkistan. The Bukharan Jews of Central Asia trace their ancestry to the Issachar and Naphtali. Isolated from centers of Jewish life, they preserved their religious identity for over twenty-seven hundred years. Since the fall of the Soviet Union, nearly all have emigrated, principally to the United States and Israel. When explorers and missionaries first made contact two hundred years ago, they found that the Bukharan Jews knew only three books of the Hebrew Bible: Genesis, Exodus, and Numbers, indicating that their knowledge and practice of the faith had declined greatly over the centuries. If they descend, as they claim, from Naphtali, their Bible of three books (Triateuch rather than Pentateuch) would reflect the biblical canon at the time of their deportation in 722 BC.

The Samaritans, separated from the Jews at the time of the return in 500 BC, had only the Pentateuch. So, it seems that Leviticus and Deuteronomy were recognized as inspired works and added to the Hebrew canon of Scripture between 700 and 500 BC. The Bukharan Jews found enough material in just the three books of the Bible that they had to keep their faith alive in conditions of remotest exile. Tobit was a contemporary of Hosea, Isaiah and Micah, the first of the writing prophets. So, all Tobit had was the Torah, and maybe only three of those first five books.

An Angel of Healing—In Catholic tradition, angels sometimes guard whole nations, and not just individuals. If the Tribe of Naphtali had a guardian angel, it would seem to have been the Archangel Raphael. Tobit's son Tobias traveled in the company of the archangel, at the archangel's bidding prayed on his wedding night to overcome demonic forces, and returned to his parents with the reserve funds along with fish gall to cure Tobit's blindness. Only then did the Archangel Raphael revealed his identity and explain the importance of righteousness, prayer and almsgiving. This angel was an answer to prayer for the common hopes and not just the individual needs of these people. For intercessors, wondering if their prayers do any good, Raphael gives assurance. *"I am Raphael, one of the seven holy angels who present the prayers of the saints and enter into the presence of the glory of the Lord"* (Tobit 12:15). God hears the prayers of the strangers and sojourners who wander about, exiled in this world, longing for their heavenly home.

Saint Raphael the Archangel

Saint Raphael is presented to us, above all in the Book of Tobit, as the angel to whom is entrusted the task of healing. When Jesus sends his disciples out on a mission, the task of proclaiming the Gospel is always linked with that of healing. The Good Samaritan, in accepting and healing the injured person lying by the wayside, becomes without words a witness of God's love. We are all this injured man, in need of being healed. Proclaiming the Gospel itself already means healing in itself, because man is in need of truth and love above all things.

The Book of Tobit refers to two of the Archangel Raphael's emblematic tasks of healing. He heals the disturbed communion between a man and a woman. He heals their love. He drives out the demons who over and over again exhaust and destroy their love. He purifies the atmosphere between the two and gives them the ability to accept each other for ever. In Tobit's account, this healing is recounted with legendary images. In the New Testament, the order of marriage established in creation and threatened in many ways by sin, is healed through Christ's acceptance of it in his redeeming love. He makes marriage a sacrament: his love put on a cross for us, is the healing power, which in all forms of chaos offers the capacity for reconciliation, purifies the atmosphere and mends the wounds.

The priest is entrusted with the task of leading men and women ever anew to the reconciling power of Christ's love. He must be the healing "angel" who helps them to anchor their love to the sacrament and to live it with an ever renewed commitment based upon it. Secondly, the Book of Tobit speaks of the healing of sightless eyes. We all know how threatened we are today by blindness to God. How great is the danger that with all we know of material things and can do with them, we become blind to God's light. Healing this blindness through the message of faith and the witness of love is Raphael's service, entrusted day after day to the priest and in a special way to the Bishop. Thus, we are prompted spontaneously also to think of the Sacrament of Reconciliation, the Sacrament of Penance which in the deepest sense of the word is a sacrament of healing. The real wound in the soul, in fact, the reason for all our other injuries, is sin. And only if forgiveness exists, by virtue of God's power, by virtue of Christ's love, can we be healed, can we be redeemed.

Pope Benedict XVI Emeritus, *Homily,* September 29, 2007

1. Describe the marital quarrel found in Tobit 10:1–7.

2. What different hopes did Tobias and his father-in-law have? Tobit 10:7–10

3. How did Raguel send off his daughter Sarah? Tobit 10:11–12

4. What did Edna say to her son-in-law Tobias? Tobit 10:13

* What blessing and advice could you offer to a newly married couple?

5. How did Tobias set out on his way? Tobit 11:1

6. What did Tobias do for his in-laws? Tobit 11:1b

7. Explain the suggestion that Raphael made. Tobit 11:2–4

8. Who else accompanied Tobias and Raphael on their journey?

Tobit 5:16	
Tobit 11:3	

9. Identify a similar sentiment expressed by two different parents.

Genesis 46:29–30	
Tobit 11:5–6, 9	

10. How would God the Father relate to a lost child coming home? Luke 15:20

* Have you or any of your loved ones ever experienced coming back home after being away from the Church or your family for a long time?

11. What advice does Raphael give Tobias? Tobit 11:7–8

12. What did Tobias do for Tobit? Tobit 11:10–13

13. Describe Tobit's response to the recovery of this sight. Tobit 11:14

* Have you ever witnessed a miraculous healing? Please describe this briefly.

14. What can you learn from the following passages?

Deuteronomy 32:39
1 Samuel 2:6
Tobit 11:15

15. How did Tobit greet his daughter-in-law? Tobit 11:16–18

16. What did Tobit want to do for Raphael? Tobit 12:1–5

* How would you try to thank someone who has helped you in a big way?

17. What advice does Raphael give them?

Tobit 12:6–7
Tobit 12:8–10
CCC 1434

18. Explain the spiritual beings created by God in these passages.

Tobit 12:11–15
Luke 1:19
Revelation 8:2
Revelation 11:7
CCC 336

19. Why did the Archangel Raphael come? Tobit 12:18

20. What did Raphael direct them to do? Tobit 12:20–22

* Do you pray to your Guardian Angel? Write a prayer to your Guardian Angel.

CHAPTER 4

The Good Book
Tobit 13–14

"Let my soul praise God the great King.
For Jerusalem will be built with sapphires and emeralds,
her walls with precious stones,
and her towers and battlements with pure gold."
Tobit 13:15–16

The Good Book—Tobit possesses many fine literary qualities, displays a rare historical perspective, and contains important teachings on several theological subjects. Although the tribe of Naphtali may have disappeared from history, they left behind this fine documentary record of their way of life, while in exile.

Authorship—At the end of the book, the Archangel Raphael instructs Tobit and Tobias to write down the story of their lives. Other biblical authors received similar instructions, to write down the message—Isaiah in the Old Testament, and John the author of Revelation in the New Testament. Some of the biblical authors, like Jeremiah, were illiterate themselves, and needed to hire a scribe to write down their message. Other important figures, like the prophets Elijah and Elisha, neither wrote anything themselves nor enlisted the help of anyone else to do so.

Tobit dictates the first two chapters himself in the first person singular, and this section concludes with his prayer at the beginning of chapter three. That was his own personal, private prayer, overheard by no one. No one but Tobit himself would have the right to record a statement like: *"For it is better for me to die than to live"* (Tobit 3:6). If he is telling the story in his own words, then the statement rings true as an honest expression of emotion. If someone else puts these words into his mouth instead, then the statement turns Tobit into a caricature. The statement follows so much fine detail, spanning all the phases of Tobit's life up to that point that one wants to believe in its authenticity. Tobit's account is one of the finest early examples of the genre of autobiography. At a time when whole nations as well as individuals were being caught up and crushed by the impersonal forces of history, Tobit's personhood, and the integrity of his individuality, constitutes a reaffirmation of human dignity.

With true genius, the author shifts from Tobit's prayer to the prayer of Sarah. The whole point-of-view of the narration shifts. No longer is Tobit the speaker, and no longer is his life the main subject. The historical plane shifts to a higher, spiritual one. Now the demons are unmasked. Demons, of course, were quite active in the life of Tobit, but also in the life of Sarah. Tobit had spent sixty years being chased from one exile to another, first exiled to Nineveh, then exiled from it, and then exiled from light. Sarah had spent a miserable decade or more watching seven men in succession die in her arms, slain by a jealous demon. These two souls, Tobit and Sarah, approach despair simultaneously, but they have many differences. They live in different countries, one male, the other female, and of different generations. Sarah is the age of Tobit's son, not of Tobit himself. But, there is a spiritual link between them. The author, who completed the rest of Tobit 3, was surely not Tobit, but the author could have been his son Tobias or Sarah.

Tobit 4 then shifts into the story of Tobias. The kind of detail, like the dog setting out with Tobias and returning with him, indicates an autobiography narrated in the third person. Just as Tobit was present at everything described in Tobit 1–3:6, so Tobias is present at all the events in Tobit 4:3–9:3. Raphael reveals his identity in an autobiographical sketch in Tobit 12:6–20. No one could have known the information shared by the archangel, but the Archangel Raphael himself.

The close of the book, which tells of Tobias' death, could only have been written by another hand, who could be called the editor. Someone collected the writing of Tobit and that of Tobias and combined them through the excellent devise of the double prayers in Tobit 3. That was probably the same person who wrote the concluding verses of the book. The most likely candidate for editor known to us is Sarah herself, the only eyewitness to her own prayer in chapter three.

Structure of the book—A framing device found in the book of Tobit is the advice that Tobit gives his son before his journey (Tobit 4:2–21), and before his impending death (Tobit 14:3–11). One should also note the device of prayers that moves the action at five critical places in the narrative:

Prayers that Move the Action

➢ Tobit prays (Tobit 3:2–6)
➢ Sarah prays (Tobit 3:11–15)
➢ Tobias prays (Tobit 8:5–7)
➢ Raguel prays (Tobit 8:15–17)
➢ Tobit prays (Tobit 13:1–18)

Tobit has the first and the last prayer, because this is his book first of all. But the book belongs in the second place to Tobias, so he gets the pivotal central prayer. Sarah and her father Raguel pray at even-numbered positions to create the sense of a whole family at prayer. Tobit's first prayer starts with the less common opening: *"Righteous are you, O Lord"* (Tobit 3:2). The rest of the prayers follow the traditional pattern: *"Blessed are you, O Lord"* (Tobit 3:11) or, *"Blessed are you, O God"* (Tobit 8:5, 15; 13:1). In the Psalter, that formula appears at the end of seven psalms (Psalm 41, 66, 68, 72, 89, 106, 135), probably an older usage, but the formula moves to an initial position in later

Jewish prayers. Tobit most beautifully uses this formula when he meets his daughter-in-law Sarah for the first time. *"Blessed is God who has brought you to us, and blessed are your father and your mother"* (Tobit 11:17). There is an expanded version of this verse in another manuscript tradition: *"Blessed be your God for bringing you to us, daughter! Blessed are your father and your mother. Blessed is my son Tobiah, and blessed are you, daughter!"* (Tobit 11:17 NAB). The sequence is interesting in that translation—blessing God first, parents second, and then the newlyweds, and in that way placing their happiness within the context of the divine plan, with which the family has been blessed from generation to generation.

Manuscript traditions—The existence of two versions of Tobit 11:17 illustrates some of the difficulty in establishing the text of Tobit. Ancient manuscripts of Tobit exist, entire or in fragments, in Hebrew, Aramaic, Greek, Latin, Syriac, Coptic, Ethiopic, and Armenian. The most ancient documents of Tobit are five fragments found at Cave Four of Qumran (4QTob). Caves Three and Four contained the largest cache of scrolls, but in very fragmentary condition. One of the Tobit fragments is in Hebrew (4Q196), and four are in Aramaic. All of these fragments come from the last two chapters of the book. There are two complete Greek-language versions (Tobit BA and Tobit S). Tobit S usually carries more detail, for example, a description of the Pentecost menu that includes "lots of little fish" (Tobit S 2:2). Tobit has an extra phrase after the last verse of the book: "and he praised the Lord God for ever and ever" (Tobit S 14:15).

In his preface to Tobit, Saint Jerome explains that he had access only to an Aramaic text, which a Rabbi orally translated into Hebrew, so that Jerome could translate it into Latin. Jerome admits to translating the entire book in one day. Jerome's version generally follows Tobit BA, but sometimes includes extra material from his source, for example: "The demon has power over those who take a wife, when they exclude God from themselves and their minds, and in this way release their libido, like horse and mule, which have no understanding" (Tobit 6:17 Vulgate). Here the archangel is quoting from the Psalter: *Be not like a horse or a mule, without understanding, which must be curbed with bit and bridle, else it will not keep with you* (Psalm 32:9).

Considering the traumas that people themselves were going through during the time of Tobit, it is a wonder that the book has been transmitted as well as it has been. The book exists in so many different languages because the literature stayed with the people during their wanderings in exile. Tobit spoke Hebrew, but Aramaic was the administrative language of the Persian Empire, and Greek of the Hellenistic and Roman Empires. As Rome was falling, one set of scholars translated the Bible into Syriac, while Saint Jerome rendered it into colloquial Latin, which most people spoke, and in which form the Roman Catholic Church preserved it for fifteen hundred years. With each shift of culture and language, the book and the people moved forward toward us, the readers. The people must have thought it was a good book.

Canonicity of Tobit—The Rabbis did not include the Book of Tobit in the Hebrew canon of Scripture in the late First Century. Their motives remain unknown to us. The Book of Tobit illustrates an important perspective not clear from other historical texts—the experience of the exile itself. Theologically, nothing in Tobit contradicts the teachings of the Torah or the Prophets. The book does not frequently quote other Old Testament writing, but there is one very pertinent quotation from the Prophet Amos: *"I will turn your feasts into mourning, and all your songs into lamentation"* (Amos 8:10; Tobit 2:6).

Tobit scholars, like David Noel Freedman and Carey A. Moore favor the opinion that the original language of Tobit was Aramaic rather than Hebrew. If Aramaic was the version known to the Rabbis, then that would have been sufficient reason for them to rule against including the book in the Hebrew Bible.

New Testament authors never quoted the Book of Tobit. However, the New Testament never quotes the Book of Nahum either, and the canonicity of that book has never been questioned. Tobit is quoted in the very early document the Didache (The Teaching of the Twelve Apostles, line 112). Most of the early Greek Fathers of the Church excluded the book from their lists, except for Clement of Alexandria, John Chrysostom and Junilius. But, most of the early Latin Fathers, including Hippolytus, Hilary, Augustine, and Cassiodrous accepted its canonicity. Since the Council of Trent in AD 1546 decreed the official list of the books of the Bible, including Tobit, the question of the canonicity of Tobit has been settled for Catholics. The subsequent discovery of Hebrew and Aramaic fragments of Tobit at Qumran has reinforced the Catholic position. Tobit is not a medieval forgery, but rather a truly ancient text, inspired by the Holy Spirit for our edification.

The Book of Tobit in Art—The popularity of Tobit emerges in the history of art. Artists assumed that patrons knew the narrative of Tobit well enough to recognize specific scenes. In 1860 William-Adolphe Bougeureau painted a scene of Tobias saying farewell to his father, with his mother weeping in the background. Jan van Scorel, Pieter Lastman, Corrado Giaguinto, Andrea del Verrochio, and Antonio Pollaiuolo all painted the fish catching in the Tigris. Jan Steen painted the signing of the marriage contract. Nikolaus Knupfer and Jan Steen painted Tobias and Sarah at prayer on their wedding night. Bernardo Strozzi painted the healing of Tobit. Rembrandt van Rijn, while still a young painter, showed interest in the latter part of Tobit. In 1632 he painted Tobit and Anna waiting for the return of their son, and in 1637 Raphael's return flight to heaven after completing his mission. Again and again, the archangel, the dog, and the fish recur in most of these paintings, so that they rise to the status of iconographic symbols.

The most moving of these artistic portrayals show departures, journeys, and returns. Anna weeps when Tobias departs. She herself had once left her childhood home to go into exile, never to return. She weeps again when he returns, because she had not dared hope she would ever see her son again. Anna's tears and the prayers of those suffering in exile ascended to heaven to the throne of God. And the story of her tears inspired a people to pray for return from exile.

The story is set among the exiled Israelites of Niniveh. The sacred author, writing centuries later, looks to them as an example of brothers and sisters in the faith dispersed among a foreign people and tempted to abandon the traditions of their fathers. The portrait of Tobit and of his family is offered as a programme of life. Here is the man who, despite everything that happens to him, remains faithful to the norms of the law, and in particular, to the practice of giving alms. He is stricken with misfortune with the onset of poverty and blindness, but his faith never fails. God's response was not slow in coming, through the Archangel Raphael, who leads the young Tobias on a risky journey, guiding him to a happy marriage and, in the end, healing his father Tobit from his blindness. The message is clear: Those who do good, above all, by opening their hearts to the needs of their neighbors, are pleasing to the Lord, even if they are tried; in the end they will experience his goodness.

With this premise, the words of our hymn can make a strong point. They invite us to lift up our eyes on high to *God who lives forever,* to his kingdom, which *lasts for all ages.* From this contemplation of God, the sacred author can offer a short sketch of a theology of history in which he tries to respond to the question which the dispersed and tried People of God are raising: why does God treat us like this? The response turns both to divine justice and mercy: *He chastises you for your injustices, but he will show mercy towards all of you* (Tobit 13:5) . . .

To sinners who are chastised for their injustices, Tobit's hymn directs a call for conversion that opens the wonderful prospect of a "reciprocal" conversion of God and man: *When you turn back to him with all your heart, to do what is right before him, then he will turn back to you, and no longer hide his face from you* (Tobit 13:6). The use of the word "conversion" for the creature and for God speaks volumes, even though it is with different meanings. If the author of the Canticle thinks of the benefits which accompany the "return" of God, his renewed favor towards his people, in the light of the mystery of Christ, we must think above all of the gift which consists of God himself. The human person has need of him more than of all of his gifts. Sin is a tragedy not just because it draws God's punishments on us, but because it banishes Him from our hearts.

The Canticle raises our eyes to the face of God as Father, inviting us to bless and praise him: *He is the Lord, our God, our Father.* One feels the sense of being special children which Israel experienced with the gift of the covenant and which prepared for the mystery of the Incarnation of the Son of God. Then, in Jesus, the face of the Father will shine forth and his mercy without limits will be revealed.

Blessed John Paul II, *General Audience,* July 25, 2001.

1. Find a common theme in the following passages.

1 Chronicles 29:10
Tobit 3:11
Tobit 8:5
Tobit 13:1

2. What can you learn from these verses?

1 Samuel 2:6
Tobit 13:2
Psalm 78:33–39
Wisdom 16:13
CCC 269

3. How should you witness to God's goodness? Tobit 13:3–4

* Share a time when you told someone about God's power.

4. Why does God punish? Tobit 13:5

5. Explain the activity in Tobit 13:6.

** How can you turn back to God? When was your last confession?

6. List the verses in which you find the word "mercy." Tobit 13–14

7. Use the Catechism or a dictionary to define "mercy." CCC 1422, 1829

*** List some ways that you have shown mercy to others who have offended you.

8. What can you learn from these verses?

Tobit 13:9	
Micah 7:19	
Revelation 21	

9. What will God do in these passages?

Tobit 13:10	
Isaiah 44:26	
Amos 9:11–15	

10. What common activity occurs in the following passages?

Tobit 13:11	
Matthew 2:1–2, 10–12	

11. Why should you bless and build up the Jews? Tobit 13:12

12. Compare the following verses.

Tobit 13:13–14
Psalm 122:6
Isaiah 66:10–12

13. How do you personally praise God? Tobit 13:15

14. Compare the following verses.

Tobit 13:16–18
Isaiah 54:11–13
Revelation 21:10–21

15. How old was Tobit when he went blind? Tobit 14:1–2

16. How long did Tobit suffer blindness? Tobit 14:1–2

17. What did Tobit do when he had grown very old? Tobit 14:3–5

18. What did Tobit foretell that the Gentiles would do? Tobit 14:6–7

19. Find four things that Tobit asked Tobias to do. Tobit 14:8–11

* Which of the above things could you do? Why are funerals important?

20. What did Tobias do in his later years? Tobit 14:11–15

"The Healing of Tobit"

Jan Massijs (1509-1575)

Monthly Social Activity

This month, your small group will meet for coffee, tea, or a simple breakfast, lunch, or dessert in someone's home. Pray for this social event and for the host or hostess. Try, if at all possible, to attend.

Think about a good person, a good family, a good parish, a good community. Now think about yourself, your own family, your own parish and share one good thing about each.

Examples

◆ *I am a good person, in that I am honest and faithful. I love God and my family, honor my word and do what I have promised to do to the best of my ability.*

◆ *My family is good in that we love and serve God, help one another, and reach out to those in need. We might not have much, but every month we set aside something for the hungry and we bring canned goods to the food pantry.*

◆ *My parish is good in that we worship God, and are faithful to the Magisterium. We enjoy solid, orthodox preaching and teaching. We have a good CCD program and an excellent RCIA program. Each Easter, we welcome new members coming into the Church.*

Chapter 5

Fear and Danger
Judith 1–7

The people of Israel cried out to the Lord their God,
for their courage failed,
because all their enemies had surrounded them
and there was no way of escape from them.
Judith 7:19

The book of Judith comes down to us only in the Greek, as no Hebrew or Aramaic manuscripts have been found. A resident of the Holy Land wrote this book in the first century BC, during the period of the Maccabean revolt. Judith loosely recounts some events, which can be identified over five preceding centuries. The literary genre could be seen as a morality play, or a free parabolic representation of historical events. Many historical, chronological, and geographic inconsistencies in the book suggest that the author did not intend to write an historical account, but rather meant to inspire readers to trust in God and remain faithful to the covenant, despite adversity. Nevertheless, the lengthy genealogy of Judith with sixteen ancestors (Judith 8:1), the longest genealogy of a woman in the Old Testament, and the reference to the exact date when Jerusalem fell to Nebuchadnezzar (Judith 2:1) indicate that there are many historical underpinnings to the narrative.

In the eighteenth year, on the twenty-second day of the first month, there was talk in the palace of Nebuchadnezzar king of the Assyrians about carrying out his revenge on the whole region, just as he said (Judith 2:1). The eighteenth year refers to 587 BC when Jerusalem actually did fall to Nebuchadnezzar. Whereas, the twenty-second day of Nisan is the day after Passover ends. In this way, the author reminds the reader of Israel's most terrible defeat on the one hand, and God's greatest deliverance of Israel from slavery in Egypt during the Exodus, commemorated on Passover, on the other. Nebuchadnezzar represents the powerful enemies of God's people. He is a dramatic and representative characterization of evil and wickedness, claiming to see himself like a god.

Judith, whose name is derived from Judah, and means "Jewess," could represent all holy women and humble people who depend completely on God, and yet take the initiative to act heroically. Her piety, wisdom, and courage are reminiscent of Miriam, who sang the praises of God after the Exodus (Exodus 15:20–21), Deborah who encouraged Barak to fight for Israel (Judges 4:4–9), and Jael, who with a tent-peg, bravely dispatched Sisera, the enemy of Israel (Judges 4:17–22).

The book of Judith also calls to mind the story of David and Goliath. Several similarities emerge in these narratives. In both cases, there is reason for the people of Israel to fear a significant enemy. In each case, God uses someone young or weak to thwart the evil plans of the powerful. God shows that He will defend the weak and vulnerable who trust in Him. Note some similarities between Judith and David:

Judith	David
She was beautiful in appearance and had a lovely face (Judith 8:7).	*He was but a youth, ruddy and comely in appearance* (1 Samuel 17:42).
Judith cried out to the Lord with a loud voice (Judith 9:1).	*"I come to you in the name of the LORD of hosts, the God of the armies of Israel"* (1 Samuel 17:45).
. . . the Lord who crushes wars, the Lord is your name (Judith 9:7).	*. . . the battle is the LORD'S and he will give you into our hand* (1 Samuel 17:47).
She . . . took down his sword . . . and said "Give me strength this day, O Lord God of Israel!" . . . and severed his head from his body (Judith 13:6–8).	*David ran and stood over the Philistine, and took his sword and drew it out of its sheath, and killed him, and cut off his head with it* (1 Samuel 17:51).

Like any good narrative, the story begins with a crisis. War is imminent. A powerful ruler and huge army march out against neighboring people, seizing their lands through warfare. Many lands are conquered, and some nations surrender without a fight. Some people prefer to go into slavery under a ruthless leader, rather than face an untimely death. *Then he came to the edge of Esdraelon, near Dothan, fronting the great ridge of Judea* (Judith 3:9). Esdraelon is a familiar place of battle for the Jewish people. During the time of the judges, Sisera the Canaanite threatened Israel in this very place at the Wadi Kishon in the valley of Esdraelon. In this place Jael killed Sisera, driving a tent-peg through his temple (Judges 4:17–23). Also, King Saul and his son Jonathan died on Mount Gilboa in this vicinity (1 Samuel 31).

Who is the God of the world? And, who will fight for Israel? Nebuchadnezzar acts as if he is a god. *"Thus says the Great King, the lord of the whole earth"* (Judith 2:5). It is profound arrogance and blasphemy to refer to oneself as the lord of the whole earth. Later he says: *"For as I live, and by the power of my kingdom, what I have spoken my hand will execute"* (Judith 2:12). Faithful Jews recognize that *as I live* is a phrase that God Almighty uses to refer to Himself, as He spoke to Moses: *"For I lift up my hand to heaven, and swear, As I live for ever"* (Deuteronomy 32:40). Furthermore, God alone has the power of life and death in His own hands. *"I kill and I make alive; I wound and I heal; and there is none that can deliver out of my hand"* (Deuteronomy 32:39). God alone is God, He and none other.

"Judith"

Georgio da Castelfranco (1477-1510)

Israel will not surrender—While other nations surrender to Holofernes, chief general of Nebuchadnezzar's army, the Israelites will not surrender. *For they had only recently returned from the captivity, and all the people of Judea were newly gathered together, and the sacred vessels and the altar and the temple had been consecrated after their profanation* (Judith 4:3). After returning from exile, they must protect their most precious possession, the temple. In this way, Judith may represent Israel, identifying with the very heart of Judaism—the temple. Joakim the high priest orders the people to seize the passes into the hills, in order to stop the invaders from advancing. And the priest and people begin to fast and pray fervently.

The people of Israel humble themselves with prayer, fasting and penance—Men, women, and even the children were praying to God for deliverance. *So the Lord heard their prayers and looked upon their affliction; for the people fasted many days throughout Judea and in Jerusalem before the sanctuary of the Lord Almighty* (Judith 4:13). The reader knows that God will be victorious. The remaining question is—how will God rescue His people from their very real fears and danger?

Meanwhile, in the Assyrian camp, an unlikely person gives a prophecy from God. Achior, leader of the Ammonites, provides a prescient report of Israel's situation. When they are faithful to God, they prosper. God protects them. When the people sin and fall away from God, their enemies defeat them. The people refuse to listen to Achior and blaspheme as well: *Who is God except Nebuchadnezzar?* (Judith 6:2). So, they bound Achior and left him lying at the foot of the hill, where he was rescued by the men of Israel and reported all that had taken place.

The enemy seizes the springs that provide water to the Israelites—Holofernes orders his whole army, one hundred and seventy thousand infantry and twelve thousand cavalry to march against Israel. When Israel sees the vast numbers coming against them, they are understandably terrified of the imminent and pressing danger. And then on the second day of the campaign, the water sources were seized. *So thirst will destroy them, and they will give up their city… they and their wives and children will waste away with famine, and before the sword reaches them they will be strewn about in the streets where they live* (Judith 7:13, 14).

The whole Assyrian army surrounds them for thirty-four days. Their cisterns were going dry. Women and children fainted from thirst. They had no strength left. The situation was desperate. Uzziah asked the people to hold out for five more days. Hopefully, God would deliver Israel at the end of the thirty-nine days. This number, just shy of forty days, should recall the traditional number *forty* for affliction. Moses fasted forty days on Mount Sinai (Exodus 34:28). Israel wandered forty years in the wilderness (Deuteronomy 29:5). The duration of Judith's widowhood (Judith 8:4) was three years and four months, which equals forty months of mourning.

The people of God cry out in their distress—When fear and danger press in, the faithful people cry out to God. In times past, when the people of Israel were in bondage to slavery in Egypt, they cried out to the Lord in their distress. *And the sons of Israel groaned under their bondage, and cried out for help, and their cry under bondage came up to God. And God heard their groaning, and God remembered his covenant with Abraham, with Isaac, and with Jacob* (Exodus 2:23–24).

The people of Israel cried out to the Lord their God, for their courage failed, because all their enemies had surrounded them and there was no way of escape from them (Judith 7:19). The term *cried out* appears ten times in the book of Judith (Judith 4:9, 12, 15; 5:12; 6:18; 7:19, 23, 29: 9:1; and 14:16). The people pray and cry out to God for deliverance. The only solution that Uzziah can imagine is rainfall, which would be a miraculous occurrence because it is not the season for rain.

In their thirst and fear and discouragement, the people implore Uzziah to surrender. They reason that it would be better to be slaves, to go back into captivity than to see their women and children die of thirst or starvation. The people became depressed.

Fear is a natural dimension of life. In childhood we experience forms of fear that subsequently are revealed to be imaginary and disappear; other fears emerge later which are indeed founded in reality; these must be faced with human determination and trust in God. However, especially today, there is a deeper form of fear of an existential type and which sometimes borders on anguish: it is born from a sense of emptiness, linked to a certain culture permeated with widespread theoretical and practical nihilism.

In the face of the broad and diversified panorama of human fears, the Word of God is clear: those who "fear" God "are not afraid." Fear of God, which the Scriptures define as "the beginning of knowledge" coincides with faith in him, with sacred respect for his authority over life and the world.

To be without "fear of God" is equivalent to putting ourselves in his place, to feeling we ourselves are lords of good and evil, of life and death. Instead, those who fear God feel within them the safety that an infant in his mother's arms feels (cf. Psalm. 130:2). Those who fear God are tranquil even in the midst of storms for, as Jesus revealed to us, God is a Father full of mercy and goodness. Those who love him are not afraid: *There is no fear in love,* the Apostle John wrote, *but perfect love casts out fear. For fear has to do with punishment, and he who fears is not perfected in love* (1 John. 4:18).

Believers, therefore, are not afraid of anything because they know they are in the hands of God, they know that it is not evil and the irrational which have the last word, but rather that the one Lord of the world and of love is Christ, the Word of God Incarnate, who loved us to the point of sacrificing himself for us, dying on the Cross for our salvation. The more we grow in this intimacy with God, imbued with love, the more easily we overcome any form of fear.

Pope Benedict XVI Emeritus, *Angelus,* June 22, 2008.

Fear and danger are common to all people. Fear of disease, financial distress, unemployment, family crises, advancing age, vulnerability, abandonment, or betrayal—any of these fears can plague contemporary people. The best way to deal with real or imagined fears, and genuine or probable danger is to cry out to the Lord in prayer, fasting and penance, just as the people of Israel did. God is rich in mercy. His tender mercy responds to the genuine and heartfelt cry of those who find themselves in trouble or danger, and yet place their trust in God alone.

1. Describe the situation in Judith 1.

2. Explain Nebuchadnezzar's motive and plan in Judith 1:12 and 2:6–7.

3. How does Nebuchadnezzar portray himself in these passages?

Judith 2:5
Judith 2:12

4. What is the appropriate response to the true King? What is His due? CCC 2639

* Recall a contemporary situation in which a leader spoke blasphemously.

5. Can you identify who is really the Great King and Lord of the whole earth?

Deuteronomy 32:39–40
Joshua 3:11
Psalm 10:16
Psalm 50:1–4
1 Timothy 1:16–17
1 Timothy 6:14–16

* Share some ways that you find helpful in praising God.

6. How do the people of the seacoast regions respond to Holofernes in Judith 3?

7. What emotion do the people of Israel feel and why? Judith 4:1–2

** Recall a time when you felt absolutely terrified. How did you handle that?

8. Where and when is this drama taking place for Israel? Judith 4:3

9. Who takes charge of the situation and what does he command? Judith 4:6–7

10. How did the people respond to the high priest? Judith 4:8–9

11. What do the people do in the following passages?

Exodus 2:23–24
2 Samuel 12:16–17
Judith 4:9–15
Jonah 3:7–10
1 Maccabees 3:47

* Have you ever combined fasting with prayer for a special intention?

12. Explain the importance of prayer and fasting.

Mark 9:17–29
CCC 1434
CCC 1387

13. Describe some aspects of fasting.

Matthew 4:1–2
CCC 538
CCC 1438
CCC 2043

* The Code of Canon Law 1249–1250 obliges Catholics to observe Fridays as a penitential day, in commemoration of the day Jesus died. Christ's faithful abstain from meat or perform other penitential practices in memory of Christ's Passion. What do *you* do to observe each Friday as a remembrance of Christ's suffering?

14. What does Achior the Ammonite recount in Judith 5:7–16?

15. Explain Achior's understanding of God and Israel. Judith 5:17–21

16. How did they respond to this report? Judith 5:22–6:9

17. What happened to Achior? Judith 6:10–20

18. What did Holofernes do next? Judith 7:1–18

19. How did Israel respond? Judith 7:19–28

20. How did Uzziah respond to the fears of the people? Judith 7:29–32

* The people were depressed. What could people do in times of desperation?

CHAPTER 6

A Good Widow
Judith 8–16

"Do not try to bind the purposes of the Lord our God;
for God is not like man, to be threatened,
nor like a human being, to be won over by pleading.
Therefore, while we wait for his deliverance,
let us call upon him to help us,
and he will hear our voice, if it please him."
Judith 8:16–17

A widow emerges to deliver God's people—Of all the people God could work through to accomplish His mighty deeds, no one in ancient Israel would expect Him to choose a woman, especially not a widow! Judith displays a combination of piety, wisdom, beauty, and courage, distinguishing her as a woman of faith. *She was beautiful in appearance and had a very lovely face; she was prudent of heart, discerning in judgment, and quite virtuous* (Judith 8:7). Her pattern of prayer and fasting was remarkable. She fasted the forty months of her widowhood, except for sabbaths and feast days of rejoicing. She had an extensive genealogy of sixteen generations, going all the way back to Israel (Judith 8:1). Judith was a wealthy woman who feared God with great devotion. No one spoke badly about her.

Judith confronts the elders—Obviously Judith was a woman of stature, as she sent her maid to summon the elders of the city to meet with her, and they responded. She must have commanded a great deal of respect for the leaders to come to her. Judith speaks to the elders for a long time, seventeen verses (Judith 8:11–27). In this instance, she sounds very much like a theologian, explaining their plight in light of the character of God. Several faith principles are taught here in Judith's speech:

1) Do not put God to the test or try to bind Him (Judith 8:12–16).
2) God has the power to protect at any time He pleases (Judith 8:15).
3) Do not accept false guilt when you have not sinned (Judith 8:18–20).
4) Thank God in times of testing (Judith 8:25).
5) The Lord can deliver Israel in amazing ways (Judith 8:33).

Israel will see that Almighty God is more powerful than the vast armies of the world. Judith insists that the people should not despair, but put their faith in God. They must never accept false guilt for sins they did not commit. They have been faithful to God. They have not fallen into idolatry in their present generation. Judith has a plan to execute, but she only tells the elders that she will go out at night with her maid. They must allow Judith and her maid to pass in and out freely.

The prayer of Judith—One entire chapter is devoted to Judith's prayer to God. She begins by humbling herself, falling prostrate, wearing sackcloth and ashes. She cries out at the same time as the evening incense in being offered to God in the temple. Judith personally intercedes to God with four petitions.

Judith's Petitions

1) O God, my God, hear the prayer of a widow (Judith 9:4).
2) Break their strength, for the sake of your sanctuary (Judith 9:8).
3) Crush their arrogance by the hand of a woman (Judith 9:10).
4) Make everyone know that God is mighty, and that God alone protects the people of Israel (Judith 9:11).

Prayer is the underpinning of the book of Judith. Repeatedly the book recounts the Jewish people crying out to God. This book is replete with personal prayer, communal prayer, fasting, penance, and worshipping God with incense in the temple. There is no hint of idolatry or false worship. Judith knows that the people are faithful. She will not allow them to fall into scrupulosity, or take on false guilt. At other times in Israel's history, they deserved God's wrath and punishment due to idolatry and infidelity. But, now the people are whole-heartedly serving God. They want to preserve the temple and the sanctuary. Judith tells the people that they should thank God for testing them, which will result in spiritual maturity.

Judith's prayer reflects "just war" principles. The conditions for legitimate defense by military force include: 1) grave and certain harm initiated by an aggressor, 2) all other peaceful means of avoiding conflict having been exhausted, 3) a reasonable prospect of success exists, and 4) the use of arms must not produce more damage than the evil to be eliminated. Prayerful people seek God first. *Some boast of chariots, and some of horses; but we boast of the name of the* LORD *our God* (Psalm 20:7). Victory is sought for the oppressed and powerless. *The bows of the mighty are broken, but the feeble gird on strength. Those who were full have hired themselves out for bread, but those who were hungry have ceased to hunger* (1 Samuel 2:4–5).

Preparation for combat—When she finishes praying, Judith removes her sackcloth and ashes, bathes and anoints her body with precious oils and perfumes, dresses in fine garments, and adorns her hair with a tiara. The reader should not assume that Judith's beauty is merely external. Interior virtue and godly character radiate through her, illuminating her exterior beauty. Both interior and exterior beauty are gifts from God, and are pleasing to behold. *A woman's beauty gladdens the countenance, and surpasses every human desire* (Sirach 36:22). The Bible also compares physical beauty with the holy lampstand in the temple. *Like the shining lamp on the holy lampstand, so is a beautiful face on a stately figure* (Sirach 26:17).

A number of stunning women appear on the pages of the Bible. Sarah the wife of Abraham was a beautiful woman. Rachel and Rebecca were both attractive and desirable women. Esther was a striking woman. An inter-textual connection may be found between Judith and Sarah, as shown in the chart below.

Sarah	Judith
Sarah is beautiful (Genesis 12:11).	Judith is beautiful (Judith 8:7)
Foreign men admire her (Genesis 12:14).	The Assyrians and Holofernes marvel at her beauty (Judith 10:14, 19, 23).
Pharaoh is deceived (Genesis 12:12–19).	Holofernes is deceived (Judith 10:11ff).
Lust causes plagues (Genesis 12:17).	Lust results in death (Judith 12–13:8).
God afflicts Pharaoh (Genesis 12:17).	God punishes the enemy (Judith 14–15).

The battle plan unfolds—Judith intends to use her beauty, her wisdom and shrewdness to destroy the belligerent enemy of Israel. Power will be vanquished by beauty. A strong soldier will fall at the hands of a defenseless widow. Judith fashions her words in a masterpiece of irony and cunning. Look especially at the way in which Judith uses the word "lord." Holofernes assumes that the word "lord" refers to himself. But, does it? *I will tell nothing false to my lord this night* (Judith 11:5). Now, Judith commands a mastery of double speak and mixed meanings. *God will accomplish something through you, and my lord will not fail to achieve his purposes* (Judith 11:6). Whose purposes will be achieved? Which lord will not fail in achieving his plans and goals? Who is Judith speaking to and about, anyway?

Holofernes, ravished by Judith's beauty, repeatedly encourages her to take courage. He has no idea just how courageous Judith actually is! Judith proclaims that she is religious. She has brought her own food and will leave every night to pray and to seek God. Holofernes is so enthralled with Judith's beauty and wisdom that he even agrees to accept the God of Israel. *You are not only beautiful in appearance but wise in speech; and if you do as you have said, your God shall be my God* (Judith 11:23). Judith's present task is not to evangelize, but to save her people.

Guest at a banquet—Just as a banquet becomes the setting for Queen Esther's plan to save her people, so Judith uses the banquet as the venue to rescue Israel from destruction. Silver dishes with fine food and wine are offered to Judith. Wisely, she refuses them. She explains that she has brought her own food, in order not to offend God by breaking the Mosaic dietary laws. Judith's beauty is so hypnotic that *Holofernes' heart was ravished with her and he was moved with great desire to possess her; for he had been waiting for* *an opportunity to deceive her, ever since the day he first saw her* (Judith 12:16). Rather than deceiving Judith, *he* is deceived and drink does him in. He drinks more wine than he has ever consumed before. How many sins have been committed, and how many bad decisions have been made throughout the ages as a result of drunkenness?

Praying to God for strength, Judith strikes Holofernes a mortal blow, and returns to her people with his head. Great rejoicing ensues. The people praise God and Uzziah blesses Judith with a prayer that Elizabeth will later proclaim to Mary (Luke 1:42). The Roman Catholic Liturgy now applies this prayer to the Blessed Virgin Mother. *O daughter, you are blessed by the Most High God above all women on earth; and blessed be the Lord God, who created the heavens and the earth, who has guided you to strike the head of the leader of our enemies* (Judith 13:18).

The victory song of Judith, after God delivers Israel through her hand, is reminiscent of the victory songs of Moses and Miriam after God parted the Red Sea and delivered Israel from slavery under pharaoh in Egypt.

Judith's Song	Exodus Songs
Judith leads the people in thanksgiving and song (Judith 16:1).	Miriam leads the women in song and dance (Exodus 15:20).
God is the Lord who crushes wars and delivers His people (Judith 16:3).	The Lord is a warrior who redeems His people from adversity (Exodus 15:3, 13).
The enemy trembled (Judith 16:10).	Terror and dread fall on the enemy (Exodus 15:16).
Sing to God a new song (Judith 16:13).	Sing to the Lord (Exodus 15:21).

Three months of celebration follow the miraculous rescue of Israel from the hand of her enemies. Despite Judith's beauty and many men who wished to marry her, she chooses to remain a widow for the rest of her life. Judith lived to be one hundred five years old. Note that one hundred five years is also the exact length of the period of the Maccabees. The message for the people of the second century before Christ and those following is to remain faithful to God, take courage, and pray fervently. God will deliver His people from oppression. God hears the cries of His people.

Judith stunningly combines beauty, piety, wisdom and courage. She is an observant Jew, faithfully keeping the law, trusting in God, with prayer and fasting. Judith illustrates the adage: "Pray as if everything depends upon God; work as if everything depends upon you." Judith cried out to God for help. She humbled herself and fasted. And then, she took the sword in her hand, and bravely did what she had to do to save her people. May we be as prayerful and bold as Judith.

The Canticle of praise (Judith 16:1–7) is attributed to Judith, a heroine who became the pride of all the women of Israel, because it was her mission to demonstrate the liberating power of God at a dark moment in the life of his people. The Liturgy of Lauds gives us only a few verses to recite. They invite us to celebrate, to sing with a full voice, play drums and cymbals, to praise the Lord "who crushes wars."

The last expression, which defines the true countenance of God, who loves peace, introduces us into the world of ideas in which the hymn was conceived. It was about a victory which the Israelites won in a totally amazing way, a work of God who intervened to rescue them from the prospect of an impending and total defeat.

The sacred author reconstructs the event several centuries later to offer his brothers and sisters in the faith, tempted to discouragement by a difficult situation, an example that can encourage them. So he refers to what happened to Israel, when Nebuchadnezzar, irritated by this people's failure to cooperate with his expansionist plans and idolatrous claims, sent the general Holofernes with the specific order to subdue and annihilate them. No one would dare to resist him who claimed the honors of a god. His general, who shared his presumption, derided the warning he was given not to attack Israel, because it would amount to attacking God himself.

In reality, the sacred author wants to emphasize this principle, to confirm believers of his time in faithfulness to the God of the covenant: one must have confidence in God. The true enemy that Israel must fear, are not the powerful ones of the earth, but infidelity to the Lord. This is what deprives them of God's protection and makes them vulnerable. Otherwise, when they are faithful, the people can count on the power of God *wonderful in his power and unsurpassable* (Judith 16:13).

. . . Now he makes use of an unarmed woman to come to the aid of his people in trouble. Strong in faith, Judith enters the enemy camps, charms the commander with her beauty and kills him in a humiliating way. The Canticle strongly underlines this fact: *The Lord Almighty has foiled them by the hand of a woman. For their mighty one did not fall by the hands of young men, nor did the sons of Titans smite him, nor did the tall giants set upon him; but Judith the daughter of Merari undid him with the beauty of her countenance* (Judith 15:5–6).

. . . The person of Judith will become the archetype that would permit not just the Jewish tradition, but even the Christian tradition to emphasize God's preference for what is fragile and weak, but precisely, for this reason, chosen to manifest divine power. She is also an exemplary figure who showed the vocation and mission of the woman, called to be man's equal, and to play a significant role in the plan of God. Some of the expressions of the book of Judith will pass, more or less integrally into Christian tradition which sees in the Jewish heroine a prefiguration of Mary. Do we not hear an echo of the words of Judith, when Mary sings in the Magnificat: *He has put down the mighty from their thrones and raised up the humble* (Luke 1:52) . . . God puts his invincible power at the support of those who are faithful to him.

Blessed John Paul II, *General Audience*, August 29, 2001.

PRAYER

This is what prayer really is—being in silent inward communion with God. It requires nourishment, and that is why we need articulated prayer in words, images, or thoughts. The more God is present in us, the more we will really be able to be present to him when we utter the words of our prayers. But the converse is also true: Praying actualizes and deepens our communion of being with God. Our praying can and should arise above all from our heart, from our needs, our hopes, our joys, our sufferings, from our shame over sin, and from our gratitude for the good.

It can and should be a wholly personal prayer. But we also constantly need to make use of those prayers that express in words the encounter with God experienced both by the Church as a whole and by individual members of the Church. For without these aids to prayer, our own praying and our image of God become subjective and end up reflecting ourselves more than the living God.

In the formulaic prayers that arose first from the faith of Israel and then from the faith of praying members of the Church, we get to know God and ourselves as well. They are a "school of prayer" that transforms and opens up our life.

Pope Benedict XVI Emeritus, *Jesus of Nazareth,*
(New York, NY: Doubleday, 2007), 130.

1. Write a short biography of Judith. Judith 8:1–8

2. Identify some other beautiful people in the Bible.

Genesis 29:17
Tobit 6:10–12
Esther 2:7

3. Find some major themes in Judith's speech to the elders.

Judith 8:12–13
Judith 8:14–15
Judith 8:16–17
Judith 8:18–23
Judith 8:24–27

4. What solution does Uzziah envision? Judith 8:28–31

5. What can God do?

Judith 8:33–35
Job 42:1–2
Luke 1:37
Mark 9:23
Mark 10: 27

* Have you ever faced some problem that only God could fix?

6. Find some major themes in Judith's prayer.

Judith 9:1–4
Judith 9:5–6
Judith 9:7–10
Judith 9:11–12
Judith 9:13–14

7. Compare the following passages.

Judith 9:5–6
Job 38:33–35
Isaiah 46:9–13
Baruch 3:35–36

8. How did prayer develop in Old Testament times? CCC 2585

* How and when do you usually pray?

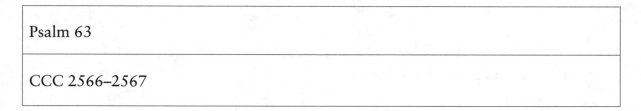

9. What is the foundation of Judith's prayer?

Judith 9:1
CCC 2559
CCC 2562

10. Who initiates prayer?

Psalm 63
CCC 2566–2567

11. Are the conditions met here to engage in a "just" war? CCC 2309

12. How do Uzziah and the elders pray for Judith? Judith 10:6–8

* How do you pray for others who ask for your prayers?

13. How do the Assyrians respond to Judith? Judith 10:11–23

** Find Judith's statements that could have a double meaning in Judith 11–12.

14. Is it ever acceptable to lie or to deceive people? CCC 2484

15. Describe the drama in Judith's conquest. Judith 12:20–13:11

16. How do the people receive Judith and how do they bless her? Judith 13:12–20

17. Explain Judith's counsel in Judith 14.

18. What does the Assyrian army do? Judith 14:11–15:7

19. Find some commonalities in the songs of Moses and Miriam, and Judith's Song.

Exodus 15:1–20	Judith 16:1–17

20. How was Judith blessed? How did she end her days? Judith 15:8-13; 16:18–25

CHAPTER 7

A Good Queen
Esther 11–12, 1–3, 13

"Think not that in the king's palace
you will escape any more than all the other Jews.
For if you keep silence at such a time as this,
relief and deliverance will rise for the Jews from another quarter,
but you and your father's house will perish.
And who knows whether you have not come to the kingdom
for such a time as this."
Esther 4:13–14

The book of Esther is a delightful book to read, but a challenging book to study. Hebrew texts of Esther, which come down from antiquity, include only Esther chapters 1–10. No mention of God is found in the entire ten chapters of the Hebrew text! God is hidden and seemingly silent. No manuscript of Esther has been discovered among the Qumran scrolls. The Greek manuscripts of the book of Esther include additions to the last chapter of the Hebrew text in Esther 10 and an additional six chapters, or one hundred seven additional verses. The Revised Standard Version Catholic Edition Bible (RSVCE) and the Jerusalem Bible (JB) indicate the Greek additions in italics. The New American Bible (NAB) displays the Greek additions by lettered designations (A, B, C, D, E, and F) rather than by chapter numbers.

The literary genre of Esther can be seen as a morality play or historical novella. Like the book of Judith, there are historical underpinnings, but there are enough historical problems to indicate that the author did not intend to write an historical work, but rather meant to impart an important moral message to his readers. The message shows that God can intervene in history to save and deliver His people from danger and from the hand of their enemies. God can use humble, lowly, helpless people—youth, orphans, refugees, or widows—to accomplish His purposes. Even though Esther is not mentioned in the New Testament, this book provides hope and inspiration for people who are discouraged, downtrodden, or in danger.

King Ahasuerus most probably is synonymous with Artaxerxes, also known as Xerxes I (reigned 485–464 BC) who lived in Susa (Nehemiah 1:1), one of the capitals of the Persian Empire. Although there is no historical reference to Mordecai, there is a secular reference to an imperial accountant in the capital of Susa during this period by the name of Marduka, who may be one and the same person. Mordecai belonged to the tribe of Benjamin, which was taken captive into Babylon by King Nebuchadnezzar (2 Kings 24:10–16; 2 Chronicles 36:10). Mordecai's genealogy includes Kish, the father of King Saul (1 Samuel 9:1) as one of his ancestors.

Mordecai's family background stands in opposition to the ancestors of Haman the Agagite. Agag was an enemy of King Saul (1 Samuel 15:8–30). God told Saul to utterly destroy the Amalekites, but Saul spared Agag the king, and was subsequently severely punished. While Haman is clearly Persian, his ancestry is traced back to an enemy of Israel. Therefore, the enmity between Mordecai and Haman is rooted in the ancient history of Israel. Haman is the antagonist in this book.

Hadassah—Esther's Hebrew name is Hadassah (Esther 2:7). Esther, the heroine, and Mordecai, the hero, are the protagonists of this biblical book. There are striking similarities between this book and the narrative accounts of Joseph (Genesis 37–50), and Daniel (Daniel 1–2). Joseph, Esther and Daniel were all exemplary Jewish youth who were taken to foreign lands, where they rose to prominent positions. Dreams are significant in all accounts. Both Joseph and Esther were influential in saving their people from imminent death. Joseph saved his people during famine, while Esther saved her people from annihilation.

The literary structure of the book of Esther involves a series of parallels and contrasts that balance one another. This literary structure is called a "chiasmus" or a chiasmic structure. Esther could be outlined as follows:

Chiasmic Structure of Esther

A. King's problem at the court (Esther 1:1–22).
B. Royal decree against the Jews (Esther 3:8–13).
C. Conflict between Mordecai and Haman (Esther 3:1–6).
* Crisis—The king's dream turns the tide (Esther 6:1–2).
C' Mordecai triumphs over Haman (Esther 6:1–7:10).
B' Royal decree favors the Jews (Esther 8:1–9:15).
A' Mordecai elevated at the court (Esther 10:1–3).

Mordecai has a dream—Mordecai's dream is recounted in the Greek prologue at the beginning of the book (Esther 11) and explained at the end of the book (Esther 10). An interesting aspect of the Greek addition echoes the prayerful lament of the book of Judith, in which Judith and the people repeatedly cried out to the Lord in prayer and fasting. *Then they cried to God; and from their cry, as though from a tiny spring, there came a great river, with abundant water; light came, and the sun rose, and the lowly were exalted and consumed those held in honor* (Esther 11:10–11). Esther is the great river that God used to bring light to the people and save them from destruction. Moredcai's discovery of the eunuch's plot to kill the king, Artaxerxes, is recounted in Esther 12:1–6 and 2:19–23, and in the king's dream in Esther 6:1–3.

Queen Vashti refuses to obey the king and embarrasses him in front of his court. The name Vashti comes from a Persian word that means "the desired one" or "the best." Subsequently, after consultation with his advisors, King Ahasuerus issues a royal decree banishing Vashti from his presence for all time. In essence, Queen Vashti was dethroned and divorced in one decree. Her royal position would then be given to another who would be deemed more worthy and docile than she was. The objective of the decree, which would be proclaimed throughout his vast kingdom, would be that *all women will give honor to their husbands, high and low* (Esther 1:20). Saint Paul reiterates this ideal in the New Testament, when he says: *Wives, be subject to your husbands, as to the Lord* (Ephesians 5:22; Colossians 3:18).

Esther is chosen as the new queen—The notion of a beauty contest to choose a queen appears in literature in the Arabian story of *A Thousand and One Nights*. Mordecai had advised Esther to keep her Jewish identity a secret. Obviously it would be easier for a Jewish girl to conceal her Jewish identity than for a Jewish boy to do so. Esther, the orphan, who was raised by Mordecai, *was beautiful and lovely* (Esther 2:7). She was placed under the care of the eunuch Hegai and underwent a year long spa treatment and beautification regime. She enjoyed six months of oil and myrrh treatments followed by six months of treatments with spices and ointments (Esther 2:12). At the conclusion of this period, she was offered whatever jewelry or accessories she desired to take with her from the harem to the palace. That Esther asked for nothing other than what Hegai advised may be an indication of her virtue of humility and docility.

Obviously the beauty treatments worked. Probably Esther was blessed with God-given natural physical attributes, which were only highlighted by the spa treatments. And, clearly there was an inner, hidden beauty of the spirit, which emanated from Esther that drew the king to her. *For from the greatness and beauty of created things comes a corresponding perception of their Creator* (Wisdom 13:5). In any event, Esther won the beauty pageant. The king experienced love at first sight: *the king loved Esther more than all the women, and she found grace and favor in his sight more than all the virgins, so that he set the royal crown on her head and made her queen instead of Vashti* (Esther 2:17). Esther becomes the new queen.

Meanwhile, the villain Haman comes onto the scene. Mordecai infuriates Haman by refusing to bow down to him. Rather than just taking his anger out on Mordecai the Jew alone, Haman seeks to destroy all of the Jews, including the women and children. During the first month of the year, the Babylonians attempted to foretell future events by means of casting lots. *Pur* means lot. The lot cast for Haman fell on the thirteenth day of the twelfth month, Adar. So, this is the day that Haman chooses to take his vengeance out on the Jews by utterly destroying them. When Haman the Agagite presents his plan to King Ahasuerus, he also offers to pay ten thousand talents of silver, a huge sum of money to destroy the Jews. The king seems somewhat detached and unconcerned as he dismissively says: *to do with them as it seems good to you* (Esther 3:11). One would hope that a monarch would be more attentive to plans involving the slaughter of one whole group of his subject peoples.

The king gives Haman authority to write a decree in his name, sealed with the king's own signet ring. Haman's letter is pompous and hostile. After claiming the king to have been *always acting reasonably and with kindness* (Esther 13:2), Haman decrees that all the Jews *shall all, with their wives and children, be utterly destroyed by the sword of their enemies, without pity or mercy* (Esther 13:6). Only four verses apart, reason and kindness are followed by annihilation without pity or mercy.

Genocide is the systematic killing of all of the people from a national, ethnic, or religious group. Unfortunately, the Jewish people have been subject to such attempts throughout history, related in the pages of the Bible and continuing to the present age. In Moses' time, the king of Egypt ordered the midwives to kill all of the baby boys born to the Hebrew women (Exodus 1:15–19). Haman proposes another such attempt at eliminating the Jews. Adolf Hitler advanced the same evil plan.

Anti-Semitism involves prejudice and hostility toward the Jews. The Second Vatican Council stated that the Catholic Church deplores all hatred, persecutions, and displays of anti-Semitism leveled at any time or from any source against the Jews. One should remember that the Jews are God's chosen people, and *he who touches you touches the apple of his eye* (Zechariah 2:8).

At a welcoming ceremony at Ben Gurion Airport in Tel Aviv, Israel in 2009, Pope Benedict XVI once again addressed the problem of anti-Semitism. He was on a pilgrimage to the Holy Land, walking in the footsteps of patriarchs and prophets, and in the setting of the events of the life, death and resurrection of Jesus Christ.

The Holy See and the State of Israel have many shared values, above all a commitment to give religion its rightful place in the life of society. The just ordering of social relationships presupposes and requires a respect for the freedom and dignity of every human being, whom Christians, Muslims and Jews alike believe to be created by a loving God and destined for eternal life. When the religious dimension of the human person is denied or marginalized, the very foundation for a proper understanding of inalienable rights is placed in jeopardy.

Tragically, the Jewish people have experienced the terrible consequences of ideologies that deny the fundamental dignity of every human person. It is right and fitting that, during my stay in Israel, I will have the opportunity to honor the memory of the six million Jewish victims of the *Shoah*, and to pray that humanity will never again witness a crime of such magnitude. Sadly, anti-Semitism continues to rear its ugly head in many parts of the world. This is totally unacceptable. Every effort must be made to combat anti-Semitism wherever it is found, and to promote respect and esteem for the members of every people, tribe, language and nation across the globe.

Pope Benedict XVI Emeritus, *Address*, May 11, 2009.

"Esther-haram"

Edward Long (1878)

1. What can you learn about Mordecai? Esther 11:2–4

2. Describe Mordecai's dream. Esther 11:5–13

3. Identify a common activity in the following verses.

Judith 5:12	
Judith 6:18	
Esther 11:10	
Esther 13:18	
Esther 10:9	
Psalm 107:6	

* What is the first thing you do when you are in trouble? What should you do?

4. What can you learn about prayer?

CCC 2604
CCC 2607–2608
CCC 2609–2611

5. What was the purpose of Mordecai's dream? Esther 11:12

6. How did Mordecai discover the plot against the king? Esther 12:1–2

7. What happened following this discovery? Esther 12:3–5

8. Why did King Ahasuerus summon Queen Vashti? Esther 1:1–11

9. What happened after the summons? Esther 1:12–19

* How should a wife respond to her husband? Ephesians 5:22–24

10. Find a common thread in these verses.

Esther 1:20
Proverbs 31:10–12
Colossians 3:18

** Share a time when you observed a woman showing great honor to her husband.

11. What can you learn about Esther? Esther 2:1–11

12. Describe Esther's beauty program. What is the source of a woman's beauty?

Esther 2:12–15
1 Peter 3:1–4

13. What happened when the king saw Esther? Esther 2:16–18

14. Find an important commandment fulfilled in these passages.

Exodus 20:12
Esther 2:20
Sirach 7:27

15. What blessing flows from this obedience? Sirach 3:3–9

* Describe an event in which an adult honored his or her father or mother.

16. How did Mordecai make Haman angry? Esther 3:1–6

** Explain a time when civil disobedience may be acceptable.

17. Explain Haman's plan. Esther 3:6; 4:6–7

18. How did Haman determine the day of execution? Esther 3:7

19. How did the king react to Haman's plan? Esther 3:8–13

20. In the King's letter, how is he described? Esther 13:2

* Define "reason." Describe a reasonable person you know.

** Explain why faith is reasonable and unbelief is unreasonable.

Chapter 8

Esther's Prayer
Esther 4, 14–15, 5–7

"O God, whose might is over all,
hear the voice of the despairing,
and save us from the hands of evildoers.
And save me from my fear!"
Esther 14:19

Mordecai learns of Haman's plot to eliminate the Jews and gets word to Esther in the palace. At first glance, it seems that Esther is reluctant to get involved. Persian royal protocol indicated that anyone who approached the throne without an invitation risked certain death. Because of the intrigue and fighting in the Middle East, access to the king was strictly controlled. After all, without adequate security measures, a spy could approach the throne and dispatch the king. Mordecai's plea comes from the Greek: *"Remember the days of your lowliness, when you were cared for by me, because Haman, who is next to the king, spoke against us for our destruction. Beseech the Lord and speak to the king concerning us and deliver us from death"* (Esther 4:8b). Hathach, the king's eunuch, has access to the women's quarters, and delivers Mordecai's request to Esther.

Esther sends back a message via Hathach to Mordecai, reminding him that anyone who approaches the king in the inner court without being summoned will be put to death. This is the law for queen and commoner alike. Apparently, the aristocracy is not exempt. Only if the king holds out his golden scepter will the intruder's life be spared. Esther isn't being capricious here. She is justifiably scared to death, and she would probably very much like to save her beautiful, regal neck!

Mordecai sends a return message to Esther. *"Think not that in the king's palace you will escape any more than all the other Jews. For if you keep silence at such a time as this, relief and deliverance will rise for the Jews from another quarter, but you and your father's house will perish. And who knows whether you have not come to the kingdom for such a time as this"* (Esther 4:13–14). Mordecai delivers some important spiritual truths in this short passage. Everyone has a time and call.

1) No one is immune from suffering, even the lofty.

2) If you disobey God's call, He can use someone else, but you will suffer.

3) God calls special people at specific times for particular tasks in life.
This is Esther's time and call.

Esther relents and calls for a fast. It should be understood that fasting without prayer is simply dieting and avails little. The Hebrew passage takes for granted that the believer will understand tacitly that both prayer and fasting are required.

Mordecai's Prayer (Esther 13:8–18)—Mordecai prays a beautiful prayer to the Lord. He praises God and explains why he would not bow down to Haman and give glory to anyone other than the Lord. He acknowledges God's power and might. He asks God to spare His people and have mercy, so that they can continue to praise His name. *"O Lord God and King, God of Abraham, God of Isaac, and God of Jacob, spare your people; for the eyes of our foes are upon us to annihilate us, and they desire to destroy your inheritance. Do not neglect your portion, which you redeemed for yourself out of the land of Egypt. Hear my prayer, and have mercy upon your inheritance; turn our mourning into feasting, that we may live and sing praise to your name, O Lord; do not destroy the mouth of those who praise you"* (Esther 13:15–17). All the people agree with this prayer.

Esther's Prayer (Esther 14:3–19)—longer than Mordecai's, echoes the prayer of her uncle, in calling on the God of her ancestors, the patriarchs. Esther's prayer becomes very personal, describing the loneliness and vulnerability of an orphan girl. *"God of Abraham, God of Isaac, and God of Jacob, blessed are you; help me, who am alone and have no helper but you . . . O Lord, my God, Come to my aid, for I am an orphan. Remember, O Lord; make yourself known in this time of our affliction, and give me courage, O King of the gods and Master of all dominion! Put eloquent speech in my mouth before the lion, and turn his heart to hate the man who is fighting against us, so that there may be an end of him and those who agree with him. But save us from the hand of our enemies; turn our mourning into gladness and our affliction into well-being"* (Esther 14:3, 11–14). Esther goes on to tell God that she hates being the queen. She abhors her lofty position. She continues to show humility and docility. Esther's prayer makes several specific points.

---

1) God keeps His promises to Israel (Esther 14:5).

2) God is righteous (Esther 14:7).

3) Death is worse than slavery (Esther 14:8).

4) God can turn their wicked plan against themselves (Esther 14:11).

5) An orphan, who has no one but God, needs courage and eloquence (14:11–13)

6) God can save us, and can turn our mourning into gladness (Esther 14:14).

Esther hosts a banquet—Banquets feature prominently in the books of this particular Bible Study. Judith attended a banquet as the guest of Holofernes (Judith 12:10–20), providing the setting for her victorious triumph over the forces of evil. King Ahasuerus and Queen Vashti were giving banquets at the beginning of the book of Esther (Esther 1:1, 9), which resulted in Vashti's banishment, and Esther's ascendancy to the throne. Later in this study, in Maccabees, you will see Simon and his sons attending a banquet and getting drunk, leading to their downfall (1 Maccabees 16:15–16). Now, Esther plans two banquets for the king and Haman. Suspense heightens as she approaches the king to issue her invitation. How will the king react to her breach of protocol? Great irony will unfold in this narrative.

When Esther approaches the king, she is probably weak from fasting from food and water for three days. Nevertheless, radiant with perfect beauty, she bravely goes through all the doors and stands before the king. His face is flushed with fierce anger. Things do not look good for Esther. Then whether from fear or weakness from fasting, Esther faints and collapses on her maid. *Then God changed the spirit of the king to gentleness, and in alarm he sprang from his throne and took her in his arms until she came to herself. And he comforted her with soothing words* (Esther 15:8). God has the power to change the hearts of kings!

The king assures Esther that she will not die. The law is only for common people, not for royalty. You cannot sue the sovereign. King and queen are above the laws governing commoners. This provides little comfort to Esther, who would lose her relative, Mordecai, all of her friends, and her entire people. Then the king makes an astonishingly generous offer. *"What is it, Queen Esther? What is your request? It shall be given you, even to the half of my kingdom"* (Esther 5:3). King Herod made a similar promise in the New Testament to the daughter of Herodias. *"Ask me for whatever you wish, and I will grant it." And he vowed to her, "Whatever you ask me, I will give you, even half of my kingdom"* (Mark 6:22–23). That promise ends disastrously for John the Baptist.

Here, Esther passes up two good opportunities to intercede for her people. And the reader does not know why. Speak up, Esther. Perhaps Esther is waiting for a prompting from God to indicate that the time is right for her to move forward, or perhaps she is afraid. Esther invites the king and Haman to a banquet that she has previously prepared, and they accept. The king again reiterates that her wish will be granted up to half his kingdom. Two narrative sets of parallelisms are shown below.

1) *What is your request? It shall be given you,*
    even to the half my kingdom (Esther 5:3).
  What is your petition? It shall be granted you. And what is your request?
    Even to the half of my kingdom, it shall be fulfilled (Esther 5:6).

2) *"If it please the king, let the king and Haman come this day to a dinner*
    that I have prepared for the king" (Esther 5:4).
  "If I have found favor in the sight of the king, and if it please the king
    to grant my petition and fulfill my request, let the king and Haman come
    tomorrow to the dinner which I will prepare for them, (Esther 5:8).

"Esther Denouncing Haman"

Ernest Norman (1859-1923)

Esther appears to be stalling. And, who could blame her? She should be terrified, and it would never hurt to butter up the king a bit. Apparently, Esther has been told that the way to a man's heart is through his stomach. She plans to make sure that the king is well fed, before she lays all of her cards on the table. In this way, the narrative creates great suspense for the irony that will soon unfold. Haman is still filled with wrath and anger against Mordecai. Despite the fact that Haman has been shown the great honor of being invited to two banquets prepared by Queen Esther for just the king and he alone, and that he has great riches, it does him no good as long as he has to look at Mordecai. Hatred and prejudice are ugly. Haman's wife Zeresh and all his friends give him the idea of constructing a high gallows on which to hang Mordecai.

The King's troubled sleep (Esther 6:1–3)—Mordecai had a dream at the beginning of the narrative, and now the king has a dream, or a case of insomnia. He reads the account of Mordecai warning the king about the plot to kill him and realizes that he never showed gratitude to Mordecai for probably saving his life. These few verses, the center of the book, provide a hinge to the narrative. From this point on, the worm turns. The plight of the Jews changes dramatically and ironically.

Arrogant Haman enters the court of the king, just as the king is considering what to do for the man whom he wants to honor. Haman conceitedly assumes that the king intends to honor himself. Haughtily, Haman suggests that the king allow the man to wear the king's robes and a royal crown, while riding upon the king's own horse. Such pride is almost unimaginable. For a subject to ride on the king's horse, wearing the king's robe and crown could be viewed as usurping the king's power. But, self-importantly Haman presses on. *Pride goes before destruction, and a haughty spirit before a fall* (Proverbs 16:18). Haman sets himself up for a very big fall.

Rather than receiving the honors that Haman has proposed, the king instructs Haman to place those honors on his enemy, Mordecai. After doing so, Haman returns home utterly disgusted, in mourning. Now, his wife Zeresh and his friends the wise men tell Haman that since he has begun to fall before Mordecai, one of the Jewish people, Haman will not prevail against his enemy, but will surely fall. How quickly the sentiments of his closest companions have changed!

Irony continues and reaches its climax during Esther's second banquet. Once again the king asks Esther's request and promises her that it will be granted, even to half his kingdom. At this point, Esther reveals that the decree to destroy the Jews includes herself, and she begs him to spare her life and the lives of her people. When the king finally hears Esther's request, he is furious because he did not realize that the plan to annihilate the Jews included his queen. Somehow the king seems to have forgotten who initiated this decree, which he approved. *And Esther said, "A foe and enemy! This wicked Haman!"* (Esther 7:6). The king flies out in a rage to his palace garden, leaving Haman and Esther alone.

When the king returns, he finds Haman has broken protocol and moved toward the queen on her couch to beg for his life. Haman has approached Queen Esther a little bit too close for comfort or propriety. The king returns to find Haman hassling the queen. One of the eunuchs in attendance advises the king that Haman has constructed a huge gallows on which to hang Mordecai. The final irony is that the king orders Haman to be hanged on the gallows he constructed for his enemy. Beware of your plans! What you wish for another may befall you!

Several lessons for personal application can be gleaned from these scriptures. One is in Mordecai's admonition to Esther: *"If you keep silence at such a time as this, relief and deliverance will rise for the Jews from another quarter . . . And who knows whether you have not come to the kingdom for such a time as this"* (Esther 4:14). There can be a big temptation to keep silent about the evils around, especially in contemporary times. It takes courage to speak up. God invites His people to take part in His plans. But, God does not need anyone. He invites, but He does not demand. Yet, in ignoring God's invitation, the blessing may be lost.

The challenge for the believer is to be docile to the Holy Spirit and discern what God calls each person to do. No believer is called to do everything. But, each person, beloved of God, is given a specific task suited to him or her. God places you in a given place, particular family, certain job, or special ministry for just such a time as this. Pray to discern God's particular call for your life.

God uses Esther, an orphan, who is weak and vulnerable. God has power. Esther does not rely on her own strengths or weaknesses. She seeks God's almighty power to direct and sustain her. She prays and fasts and then accomplishes what God has in store for her to do. We could do the same.

---

1. What did Mordecai do when he learned the news of the decree? Esther 4:1–8

2. What did Mordecai ask of Esther? Esther 4:8b

3. Why was Esther reluctant to help? Esther 4:10–12

* Do you think Esther's fears were reasonable or unfounded?

4. Explain three things that Mordecai says to Esther in Esther 4:13–14.

** Find a personal application to: *perhaps God has called you for such a time as this.*

5. How could a person discern what God is calling him or her to do? CCC 2690

6. What did Esther decide? Esther 4:15–17

7. How could you discern between trials and temptations? CCC 2847

* Who would you go to for help in discernment?

8. Write some sentiments from Mordecai's Prayer?

| Esther 13:8–9 |
| Esther 13:10–11 |
| Esther 13:12–14 |
| Esther 13:15–16 |
| Esther 13:17–18 |

9. What is the first thing that Esther did? Esther 14:1–2

10. Write some sentiments from Esther's Prayer.

Esther 14:3–4
Esther 14:5–10
Esther 14:11–12
Esther 14:13–14
Esther 14:15–19

** Write your own prayer to God for times of trouble.

11. Describe how Esther looked when she went to see the king. Esther 15:1–6

12. Explain the drama in Esther 15:7–16.

13. Find two parallelisms in Esther 5. Are there any differences?

Esther 5:3	Esther 5:4
Esther 5:6	Esther 5:8

14. Describe Haman and his wife.

Esther 5:9–10
Esther 5:11–13
Esther 5:14

15. How does the drama change in Esther 6:1–3?

* Did you ever forget to show gratitude to someone who helped you? Or vice versa?

16. Explain the drama in Esther 6:4–9.

17. Describe the irony in Esther 6:10–13.

18. What happens at Esther's second banquet? Esther 6:14–7:6

19. How does the king respond to Esther's request? Esther 7:7

20. What seals Haman's fate and completes the irony? Esther 7:8–10

* What practical wisdom can you learn from Haman's mistakes?

Monthly Social Activity

This month, your small group will meet for coffee, tea, or a simple breakfast, lunch, or dessert in someone's home. Pray for this social event and for the host or hostess. Try, if at all possible, to attend.

Think about a time when God call you for "such a time as this." You, like Esther, might have had a difficult time responding to God's call. Or, perhaps God is calling you right now to do something special for him in a specific ministry. What do you think it might be?

Examples

◆ *When a Pregnancy Counseling Center opened up in our town and I was asked to help out, I knew I had to respond and volunteer.*

◆ *When Father asked me to teach CCD, I didn't think I had the time or the patience, but I agreed. The blessings were amazing.*

◆ *There are not many programs for mothers with pre-school children, in our parish. So, perhaps God is calling me to provide childcare for Bible Study during the day, and to do my study at night.*

CHAPTER 9

God Saves the Jews
Esther 8, 16, 9–11

"And my nation, this is Israel,
who cried out to God and were saved.
The Lord has saved his people;
the Lord has delivered us from all these evils;
God has done great signs and wonders,
which have not occurred among the nations.
For this purpose he made two lots,
one for the people of God and one for all the nations.
And these two lots came to the hour and moment and day of decision
before God and among all the nations.
And God remembered his people and vindicated his inheritance."
Esther 10:9–12

God saves the Jews through Esther—The central underlying problem presented in the book of Esther is the imminent threat of annihilation of all the Jewish people in the land—men, women, and children. The Jewish people are scheduled to be annihilated, completely destroyed, by means of the sword, on the fourteenth day of Adar. After Haman's death, the king gives Esther all of Haman's property. Esther now reveals to the king her relationship with Mordecai, her uncle and guardian. At this point, the king summons Mordecai, indicating that he is being brought into the king's inner circle. The king takes off his signet ring, which he had previously given to Haman, and gives it to Mordecai. So, essentially Mordecai has supplanted Haman, becoming something like a prime minister.

Unfortunately for the Jews, Persian law is irrevocable (Esther 8:8). So, the king's edict, which Haman scripted, cannot be revoked or cancelled. Therefore, the Jews need to think of something fast. Esther no longer appears as the frightened young orphan girl relying on Mordecai for direction, but rather she emerges as a self-confident woman who knows what she must do to save her people. She must employ her considerable talents to orchestrate a favorable course of events for them.

Interestingly, Esther places all of the blame for the genocidal plan against the Jews upon Haman the Agagite. She chooses not to implicate the king in the anti-Semitic plot, which he approved. In this way, she demonstrates wisdom and diplomacy. An emotional woman might have railed against the king for allowing such a horrible edict to ever have been written at all. But, Esther chooses her words wisely and plans her battle well. *A soft answer turns away wrath, but a harsh word stirs up anger. The tongue of the wise dispenses knowledge . . . with patience a ruler may be persuaded* (Proverbs 15:1–2; 25:15). The stakes are very high for the Jewish people. Esther's diplomacy will determine whether the Jews will live or be slaughtered.

Once again, Esther approaches the king with great emotion and he holds out the golden scepter to receive her and allow her to speak. Esther petitions her husband, the king with soft and deferential words.

> *If it please the king,*
> *and if I have found favor in his sight,*
> *and if the thing seem right before the king*
> *and I be pleasing in his eyes*
> (Esther 8:5)

Esther asks that the edict written by Haman be revoked. But, the king explains to her that a decree written in the name of the king and sealed with his ring cannot be repealed. However, he summons his secretaries and allows Mordecai to compose a new declaration, allowing the Jews to defend themselves. But, they must act quickly. The date of Haman's decree, the twenty-third day of Nisan (Esther 3:12) and the time of the edict composed by Mordecai, indicates that seventy days have passed. This number recalls the seventy years of the Babylonian exile to show that this edict proposed a tragedy similar to the captivity and exile of the Jewish people under Nebuchadnezzar (2 Kings 25; Jeremiah 39:1–7; 2 Chronicles 36:20–21).

The second letter from the king (Esther 16)—Whereas the king's first letter composed by Haman sought to destroy the Jews, this second letter composed by Mordecai exonerates the Jews. The first fourteen verses of the letter expose the wickedness of Haman. Mordecai accuses Haman of undermining the authority of the king and attempting to transfer the kingdom of the Persians to the Macedonians. The next part of the letter shows the Jews to be sons of the Most High God. People are instructed to not put into execution the directives of the letter of Haman. Jews should be permitted to live under their own laws and have a right to defend themselves. So, that on the very day when the Jews would have been destroyed, they will now fight for life. *For God, who rules over all things, has made this day to be a joy to his chosen people instead of a day of destruction for them* (Esther 16:21).

The Jews had light and gladness and joy and honor (Esther 8:16). Light signifies the presence of the Lord and His protection. *The Lord is my light and my salvation; whom shall I fear?* (Psalm 27:1). The light of the Lord and His favor has once again shown upon the people of Israel. *Light dawns for the righteous, and joy for the upright in heart* (Psalm 97:11). God provides for their prosperity and wellbeing. He used Esther to bring evil plans into the light and rescue the lives of the people. Now, they experience gladness, joy and honor.

Victory for the Jews (Esther 9:1–15)—On the day when they would have been executed, the Jews go into battle and win a huge victory. The numbers of those slain are intended to show a great romp of their foes. These numbers are not intended to have an historical, literal, numerical value. But, now the tides have turned. God has saved the Jews from calamity. There is no mention of killing women and children. So, the reader may assume that this represents a traditional situation of war, regrettable as it is. Also, note in the text, that on three occasions it states that the Jews took no plunder (Esther 9:10, 15, and 16). The Jews were not interested in seizing the property of those who fought against them. The point of the battle was self-defense, preserving their lives, not taking booty. The accounts do not recount any Jewish loss of life, but in battle certainly one would expect some losses on both sides. The over-riding point is that God gave His people victory over their enemies.

The Feast of Purim (Esther 9:16–32)—The Jews institute an annual feast to recall the day when they got relief from their enemies. After the battle, the people rested. Rest is a hope, a promise and a gift from God: *for you have not as yet come to the rest and to the inheritance which the* LORD *your God gives you* (Deuteronomy 12:9). People desire rest and peace. A foretaste of rest is experienced each sabbath. However, the ultimate longing for rest and peace cannot be fulfilled in this world. Mordecai instructed all the Jews, that they should keep the feast of Purim: *enjoining them that they should keep the fourteenth day of the month of Adar and also the fifteenth day of the same, year by year, as the days on which the Jews got relief from their enemies, and as the month that had been turned for them from sorrow into gladness and from mourning into a holiday; that they should make them days of feasting and gladness, days for sending choice portions to one another and gifts to the poor* (Esther 9:21–22).

The feast of Purim, derived its name from *pur* for "lot" to recall Haman's casting of lots to determine the date of the slaughter of the Jews. But, God changed their lot to favor the chosen people. In former times, when the book of Esther was read in synagogues, the men would stomp their feet, make noise, boo Haman the villain, and cheer and applaud the heroine Esther and hero Mordecai. A big celebration with eating and drinking followed the reading. Purim became a type of carnival celebration recalling the time when the Jews triumphed over their enemies, through the intervention of a beautiful and courageous Jewish orphan, *Hadassah* (Esther).

To this day, Purim parties are celebrated in synagogues. Little Jewish girls dress up like Queen Esther and little boys dress up like Mordecai. They eat *Homentashin*—little three cornered pastries filled with poppy seeds, shaped like Haman's hat. The children are told the story of how God changed the lot of His people and gave them victory over their enemies. They cheer for Esther and Mordecai. And there is a big celebration of God's goodness for all the Jewish people.

Mordecai's Dream Fulfilled (Esther 10)—Chapter 10 of Esther shows that God was silently working behind the scenes for His people all along. Now, the faithful Jew, Mordecai is elevated in stature next in rank to King Ahasuerus. Mordecai was great because the good of his people was primary in his aims: *he was great among the Jews and popular with the multitude of his brethren, for he sought the welfare of his people and spoke peace to all his people* (Esther 10:3).

God can, and often does, change people's fortunes. *You have changed my mourning into dancing; you have loosed my sackcloth and clothed me with gladness, that my soul may praise you and not be silent. O LORD my God, I will give thanks to you for ever* (Psalm 30:11–12). God took a dangerous and fearful situation for the Jews and turned it into a time for celebrations and great rejoicing. God did this repeatedly in the history of the Jewish people, as the psalmist recalls. *When they are diminished and brought low through oppression, trouble, and sorrow, he pours contempt upon princes and makes them wander in trackless wastes; but he raises up the needy out of affliction, and makes their families like flocks. The upright see it and are glad; and all wickedness stops its mouth. Whoever is wise, let him give heed to these things; let men consider the steadfast love of the LORD* (Psalm 107:39–43).

The Greek closing of the book of Esther explains the dream of Mordecai that was recounted in the prologue. The tiny spring that became a river symbolized the little orphan girl *Haddasah* (in Hebrew), who became the valiant Queen Esther. The two dragons are the enemies Haman and Mordecai. The two dragons fought one another with great irony. The oppressed Mordecai, in danger of annihilation becomes the victor. Haman, the villainous Jew-hater is executed on the very gallows that he constructed for the Jew Mordecai. But, because of the war, there is blood on both Mordecai and Haman's hands, making Mordecai a dragon as well.

Two lots were cast—one for the chosen people and one for foreign nations. The two lots came together at a particular date that God chose for His people. God remembered and vindicated His inheritance. One should not suppose that God forgot his chosen people, in the way that humans might forget something. Rather, the dangerous situation combined with the prayer and fasting of Esther and Mordecai and the people prompted God to act on their behalf.

Celebration of the feast of Purim

1) Cultivates a strong sense of Jewish identity (Esther 9:1–17)
2) Provides a time of rest and rejoicing (Esther 9:18–19)
3) Fosters generosity in the community and a concern for the poor (Esther 9:20–28)

God can use the weak and the vulnerable to achieve His purposes. God comes to the rescue of people who pray, fast, and trust in Him. Reflect on ways that God has blessed and protected His people in contemporary times. Share stories about God providing for people during the Great Depression and during war times. Courageous women have risen up in each generation to save the lives of the innocent. Irena Sendlerowa, a Catholic social worker in Poland, ingeniously saved the lives of over twenty-six hundred Jewish children in the Warsaw Ghetto, during the Holocaust. For this she was tortured and sentenced to death. But, God protected her. Remembering the signs and wonders that God has worked in the past provides hope for present trials and strength for the future.

The family is called to work for the handing on of the faith. Esther admits: *Ever since I was born I have heard in the tribe of my family that you, O Lord, took Israel out of all the nations* (Esther 14:5). . . . None of us gave ourselves life or single-handedly learned how to live. All of us received from others both life itself and its basic truths, and we have been called to attain perfection in relationship and loving communion with others. The family, founded on indissoluble marriage between a man and a woman, is the expression of this relational, filial and communal aspect of life. It is the setting where men and women are enabled to be born with dignity, and to grow and develop in an integral manner.

Once children are born, through their relationship with their parents they begin to share in a family tradition with even older roots. Together with the gift of life, they receive a whole patrimony of experience. Parents have the right and the inalienable duty to transmit this heritage to their children: to help them find their own identity, to initiate them to the life of society, to foster the responsible exercise of their moral freedom and their ability to love on the basis of their having been loved, and, above all, to enable them to encounter God. . . .

Esther's father had passed on to her along with the memory of her forebears and her people, the memory of a God who is the origin of all and to whom all are called to answer. The memory of God the Father, who chose a people for himself and who acts in history for our salvation. The memory of this Father sheds light on our deepest human identity: where we come from, who we are, and how great is our dignity. Certainly we come from our parents and we are their children, but we also come from God who has created us in his image and called us to be his children. Consequently, at the origin of every human being there is not something haphazard or chance, but a loving plan of God. This was revealed to us by Jesus Christ, the true Son of God and perfect man. He knew whence he came and whence all of us have come: from the love of his Father and our Father.

. . . The Church at prayer has seen in this humble queen interceding with all her heart for her suffering people, a prefigurement of Mary, whom her Son has given to us all as our Mother, a prefigurement of the Mother who protects by her love God's family on its earthly pilgrimage. Mary is the image and model of all mothers, of their great mission to be guardians of life, of their mission to be teachers of the art of living and of the art of loving.

The Christian family—father, mother and children—is called, then, to do all these things not as a task imposed from without, but rather as a gift of the sacramental grace of marriage poured out upon the spouses. If they remain open to the Spirit and implore his help, he will not fail to bestow on them the love of God the Father made manifest and incarnate in Christ.

Pope Benedict XVI Emeritus, *Homily,* July 9, 2006.

1. What can you learn from the following verses?

Esther 8:1–2	
Proverbs 11:8	
Matthew 7:2	

*What common adage told from parents to children comes from these verses.

2. How did Esther approach the king and what did she ask of him? Esther 8:3–6

3. What virtues does Esther possess?

CCC 1806	
CCC 1808	
CCC 2546	
CCC 2559	

*Define virtue. Which virtue, do you most desire? How can you grow in virtue?

4. What was the king's response? Esther 8:7–8

5. Identify the major, insurmountable problem facing the Jews. Esther 8:8b

6. What was the objective of the king's second edict? Esther 8:11

7. Identify and define the deadly sin that Haman displays.

Esther 16:2–7, 12
Proverbs 16:18

** Which sin is the root sin of all other sin? CCC 1866   How can you root it out?

8. How could one grow in virtue and battle against sin? CCC 1784

* Identify one virtue and a practical means of growing in that specific virtue.

9. What does Mordecai identify as Haman's ultimate goal? Esther 16:14

10. What does Mordecai reveal about the Jews? Esther 16:15

11. What does Mordecai ask the people to do and why? Esther 16:17–21

12. How did Mordecai appear to the people? Esther 9:3–4

13. How do those people, who are rescued by the Lord react?

Esther 16:16–17
Isaiah 51:11

14. Describe the drama in Esther 9:1–11

15. What noteworthy fact is repeated about the battle? Esther 9:10, 15, 16

16. What was done on the fourteenth day of Adar? Esther 9:19

* Feasting is the opposite of fasting. How do you, as a Catholic, observe each?

17. Why was it important for the Jews to celebrate? Esther 9:20–22

18. What did they call this feast and why? Esther 9:26–32

* List times of religious celebration. How does your family celebrate these days?

19. How did Mordecai end up? Esther 10:1–3

20. Explain Mordecai's Dream. Esther 10:4–13

** How can good people resist the temptation to do nothing in the face of evil?

*** Share an example of a contemporary hero, defending the lives of others.

CHAPTER 10

The Good Prince
Ezra 1–3

And they sang responsively, praising and giving thanks to the LORD,
"For he is good, for his mercy endures for ever toward Israel."
And all the people shouted with a great shout,
when they praised the LORD,
because the foundation of the house of the LORD *was laid.*
Ezra 3:11

The return from exile was the fulfillment of yearning on the part of a whole nation, and not just the work of a single individual. As a result, the Book of Ezra is a book of many heroes, the greatest of whom happens to be the Scribe Ezra. One should note, however, that the man after whom the book is named does not appear until chapter seven. By that time, the author has introduced several other heroes who set the stage for the work of Ezra.

Cyrus of Persia—In the very first verse, the author twice mentions "Cyrus, King of Persia," the monarch who authorized the Hebrews return from exile. Although Cyrus was not Jewish himself, he holds a position of high honor in Hebrew literature. Unlike the Pharaoh of Egypt, who through his hard-heartedness had refused to let the people go, Cyrus of Persia freely liberated them. Isaiah delivers a prophetic word about Cyrus unlike any given to any other gentile ruler:

> *"I am the* LORD *. . . who says of Cyrus, 'He is my shepherd,*
> *and he shall fulfill all my purpose';*
> *saying of Jerusalem, 'She shall be built,'*
> *and of the temple, 'Your foundation shall be laid.'"*
> *Thus says the* LORD *to his anointed, to Cyrus,*
> *whose right hand I have grasped,*
> *to subdue nations before him and uncover the loins of kings,*
> *to open doors before him that gates may not be closed:*
> *"I will go before you*
> *and level the mountains,*
> *I will break in pieces the doors of bronze*
> *and cut asunder the bars of iron,*
> *I will give you the treasures of darkness*
> *and the hoards in secret places,*
> *that you may know that it is I, the* LORD,
> *the God of Israel, who call you by your name."*
> (Isaiah 44:24, 28–45:3)

At the beginning of the prophecy, the word "anointed" (Isaiah 45:1) renders the Hebrew word *Messiah*. Cyrus is a messianic figure, a foreshadowing of Jesus the Messiah, who would set the people of the whole world free from exile. In the previous verse (Isaiah 44:28), Cyrus is called "shepherd," because unlike the bad shepherds of the Assyrian and Babylonian monarchies, Cyrus promotes the good of all his people. In this way too, he foreshadows the pastoral concern of Jesus, the Good Shepherd. Cyrus does not know the God of the Hebrews, but by looking into his own heart, he finds the goodness to do what is right for God's people. Therefore, the Lord calls Cyrus by his name, and girds him for universal rule.

The Book of Ezra calls Cyrus "the King of Persia." In the Persian language, the word for king is *shah,* and the Persian monarch had the official title "Shah of Shahs," which means "King of Kings." In his own book, the prophet Daniel addresses the Persian monarch with this fuller form of his official titulary: *"You, O king, the king of kings"* (Daniel 2:36). Later, in the New Testament, this title, the King of Kings is bestowed upon Jesus (1 Timothy 6:15; Revelation 17:14; 19:16).

In original form, the title "king of kings" means "emperor," the highest ruler in a hierarchical structure of rulers, with subordinate kings accountable to him. Cyrus ruled over such a vast empire, stretching from Greece to India, that he could not administer everything personally. The Persian Empire was subdivided into provinces, each having a governor appointed by Cyrus to control local affairs.

Since the Persians absorbed the Babylonian Empire peacefully, without the need of military force, they kept in office the local officials inherited from the previous empire. Initially, the Holy Land was part of the same province as Babylon proper in the Persian system of government. They shared the same governor, who would have been called a petty king, a "minor shah."

Sheshbazzar, Prince of Judah—The second great hero introduced by Ezra is the most prominent elder of the Jewish community at the beginning of the Persian period, a man using the Babylonian name of Sheshbazzar. To this man, Cyrus hands over the temple vessels taken from the temple in Jerusalem by Nebuchadnezzar the Babylonian. He had to have been a man of high esteem with the Jewish people.

Many Jewish men were given Babylonian names during the period of their exile. Recall the new names awarded to the young men admitted to the royal school of administrative service, from the Book of Daniel. *And the chief of the eunuchs gave them names: Daniel he called Belteshazzar, Hananiah he called Shadrach, Mishael he called Meshach, and Azariah he called Abednego* (Daniel 1:7). So the man introduced as Sheshbazzar in the first chapter of Ezra (Ezra 1:8), reappears in the third chapter with his true, Hebrew name of Shealtiel (Ezra 3:2).

Shealtiel or Sheshbazzar bears the titles "prince" (Ezra 1:8) and "governor" (Ezra 2:63). As prince, he belongs to the tribe of Judah and the family of David. Two of the evangelists offer genealogies of the ancestors of Jesus, and both of them include Shealtiel among them. *And after the deportation to Babylon, Jechoniah was the father of Shealtiel, and Shealtiel the father of Zerubbabel* (Matthew 1:12). Similarly, Luke reports: *. . . the son of Joanan, the son of Rhesa, the son of Zerubbabel, the son of Shealtiel* (Luke 3:27).

The text of Ezra does not mention when Shealtiel took up the position of governor in the Holy Land (Ezra 2:63). Endowed with a Babylonian name, he probably belonged to the administrative service of that kingdom, as Daniel did. Conceivably, Shealtiel was already governor of the ghost town of Jerusalem under the Babylonians. As son of the last king Jechoniah, Shealtiel was next in line to sit on the throne of David. The imperial masters did not allow him to be crowned with the glory of official rule, but they were happy to use his position of high respect among his own people as an instrument for their own control over the population. He was not allowed to become an independent king, but he was recognized as of royal blood and of dynastic lineage, and so he was one of those "minor shahs" who served at the pleasure of Cyrus, the "Shah of Shahs."

Shealtiel was a layman, and did not have the priestly function to be able to handle the temple vessels personally. He would have reported to the treasurer with a cohort of priests belonging to the tribe of Levi. The Levitical priests were the ones who actually took physical possession of *a thousand basins of gold, a thousand basins of silver, twenty-nine censers, thirty bowls of gold, two thousand four hundred and ten bowls of silver, and a thousand other vessels; all the vessels of gold and of silver were five thousand four hundred and sixty-nine* (Ezra 1:9–11). Shealtiel was at the head of the party of exiles that brought these precious and treasured objects back to Jerusalem.

The Babylonian Exile—The period of the exile spanned a half century, from the fall of Jerusalem in 587 BC to the fall of Babylon in 537 BC. Shealtiel, the son of the last king, Jechoniah (Matthew 1:12), may have been carried to Babylon as a baby. If so, he could have been in his mid-fifties when the temple vessels were handed over to him. He would have been young enough to continue as governor for another year or two, when the governorship apparently passed on to his son and heir Zerubbabel, along with another hero of the return by the name of Jeshua.

Now in the second year of their coming to the house of God at Jerusalem, in the second month, Zerubbabel the son of Shealtiel and Jeshua the son of Jozadak made a beginning, together with the rest of their brethren, the priests and Levites and all who had come to Jerusalem from the captivity (Ezra 3:8). The torch was passed to a new generation of Israelites. Shealtiel belonged to the generation that was sent into exile; whereas, his son Zerubbabel belonged to the next generation that returned home from their exile.

During the lifetime of Shealtiel there remained a small Jewish population in the Holy Land. Even ghost towns like Jerusalem was at that time would not be completely uninhabited. The Babylonians deported the population of Israelites in three waves. First they took the elite class into captivity, then the middle class, and finally the common people. In the countryside, however, there are many caves and hiding places. The poor, who had nothing to start with, could easily slip away into one of the caves, and survive undetected for a later day. This may be the historical meaning of the beatitude *"Blessed are the meek, for they shall inherit the earth"* (Matthew 5:5, quoting Psalm 37:11).

Shealtiel may have been governor of the few poor who survived in the land, but his son Zerubbabel brought back many of the exiles—probably not the wealthy either, but those without fixed roots, property, or multiple responsibilities back in Babylon. So, the poor who were deported (counted and named in Ezra 2) came back to rejoin the poor who had escaped deportation. The work of Jeshua and Zerubbabel involved reintegrating the deportees with the local population. Working together on rebuilding the temple was a wonderful opportunity to reconstitute the community from these two groups, with vastly different life experiences. Their emotions ranged from sorrow to joy. *So that the people could not distinguish the sound of the joyful shout from the sound of the people's weeping, for the people shouted with a great shout, and the sound was heard afar* (Ezra 3:13). Major changes in life can result in a wide range of emotions. While some are sorrowful at leaving their present circumstances, others are joyful.

Let the people " . . . *rebuild the house of the Lord, the God of Israel*" (Ezra 1:3). With these words Cyrus, King of Persia, granted freedom to "the remnant of Israel" and ordered the exiles to *rebuild in Jerusalem the holy place,* where the name of God could be adored. This was a duty the exiles gladly accepted, and they set out with enthusiasm towards the land of their fathers.

We can imagine the excitement of their hearts, the haste of their preparations, the tears of joy and the hymns of gratitude which preceded and accompanied their steps as they returned to their Homeland. After the tears of the Exile, "the remnant of Israel" could laugh once again, as they hastened towards Jerusalem, the City of God. At last they could sing their songs of thanksgiving for the great wonders which the Lord had worked in their midst (cf. Psalm 126:1–2).

Similar feelings fill our own hearts today, as we celebrate this Eucharist in honor of the Blessed Virgin Mary, Queen of Peace. After the Communist oppression, you too—not unlike exiles—once more return to *proclaim together your common faith.* Today, ten years after regaining your freedom, you remember the struggles of the past and you sing praise to the provident mercy of the Lord, who does not abandon his children in their distress.

Blessed Pope John Paul II, *Homily in Kazakhstan,* September 24, 2001.

1. Who or what prompted Cyrus to act on behalf of the Jews?

2 Chronicles 36:22–23	
Ezra 1:1	

2. What does the Prophet Isaiah reveal about Cyrus?

Isaiah 44:28	
Isaiah 45:1	
Isaiah 45:2–3	
Isaiah 45:4–5	

3. In your own words, explain the good news in Ezra 1:2–4.

4. What was the response to this news? Ezra 1:5–6

5. How and why did the sacred vessels end up in Babylon? 2 Chronicles 36:9–10

6. Describe the activity in Ezra 1:7–8.

7. How many precious vessels were recovered? Ezra 1:9–11

_1,000_ *basins of gold and* _1,000_ *basins of silver* _____ *censers*		
_____ *bowls of gold,* _____ *bowls of silver* _____ *other vessels*		
All the vessels of gold and silver _____		

8. How many priests returned from exile? Ezra 2:36–39

9. Find two special categories of Levites. Ezra 2:40–42

10. What special role emerges in the census in Ezra 2:43–58?

11. Who defined and gave dignity to the role of servant? Mark 9:35

12. Identify some special ways to serve God and others.

CCC 852	
CCC 1653	
CCC 1654	

* How is God inviting you to serve right now?

13. What happened to those who could not prove their status? Ezra 2:59–63

14. How large was the whole assembly of exiles? Ezra 2:64–67

15. Describe the generosity shown in Ezra 2:68–69.

16. Where did the people returning from exile set up residence? Ezra 2:70

17. What happened in Ezra 3:1–5?

18. What problem did they face and how did they address it? Ezra 3:6–9

19. What was the response to the laying of the temple foundation? Ezra 3:10–11

20. With what emotion did the older people react? Ezra 3:12–13

* Recall a time when you responded to a situation with both joy and sorrow.

CHAPTER 11

The Good Prophets
Ezra 4–6

Now the prophets, Haggai and Zechariah the son of Iddo,
prophesied to the Jews who were in Judah and Jerusalem,
in the name of the God of Israel who was over them.
Ezra 5:1

The gift of prophecy rose to prominence in the time of the monarch, when prophets were inspired by God to nominate and anoint the ruling monarchs. No king of Israel could reach the throne, or rule successfully after ascending the throne, without the backing of the prophets. Samuel anointed King Saul and King David. Nathan anointed King Solomon, and so forth. Sometimes prophets stood in opposition to the monarch, as Elijah stood against Ahab, and in such cases the king's authority was seriously undermined by his failure to heed the prophets.

> **PROPHET** (*nabi* in Hebrew)—is the authorized spokesman of God. The prophet knows that he has been called by God, and receives a specific message from God for the people. The prophet has a clear mission to communicate, orally, in writing, or by his actions, God's message in His name as His Word.

When the kingdom finally fell and the last king left his throne, there was a period of confusion about whether the gift of prophecy had been taken away as well. Soon, however, it became clear that God was going to continue speaking, even if there was no king in the land. A new outpouring of prophecy came in the writings of the former scribe Baruch, of the major prophets, Daniel and Ezekiel, and in several of the minor prophets as well.

The term "major prophet" refers to one who left behind a large written legacy, while the term "minor prophet" simply means one who wrote a short book, easily written out on a single scroll. Two of the minor prophets, Haggai and Zechariah, not only contributed their own books, but also make an appearance in the fifth chapter of the Book of Ezra. They belong to the second wave of the return from exile. The first wave, which was led by Sheshbazzar, is followed by a second group led by his son Zerubbabel and Jeshua.

Sheshbazzar and the priests in the first group brought the temple treasures back home to Jerusalem, but, on their return, they found no suitable house of worship in which to place them. The task of the second group was to provide the house for the Lord. Haggai and Zechariah provide the people with their marching orders from God, to build the "Second Temple."

In chapter four of Ezra, the leaders reject the help offered from the local gentiles, who had been imported into the land by the Assyrians. Ezra calls them *people of the land* (Ezra 4:4), but in fact, they were foreigners exiled to Israel. Just as the Assyrians made the Israelites leave, they also made other people come. This exchange of population was part of the strategy of the "Shepherds" who ruled Asshur. The rulers hoped to interbreed the populations and extinguish the national identities of all the people, and so make them more submissive to their rule.

The Babylonians carried away the tribe of Judah, but apparently did not send in other peoples to replace them. So, the problem in intermingling existed mainly in the northern part of the Holy Land, not in the south. Also, the intermingling had occurred long before the fall of the south. For nearly a hundred and fifty years, the Judeans had looked on in horror from next door, while the genetic experiment was being conducted in the territory of the fallen northern kingdom.

The animosity between Samaritans and Jews arose not at the time of the return, but long before the fall of the southern kingdom. After the exile, the returning Jews knew that they would be facing their half-cousins in the land. The Book of Ezra gives names to some of their adversaries—the leaders Bishlam and Mithredath and Tabeel (Ezra 4:7) along with Rehum the commander, and Shimshai the scribe (Ezra 4:8). These anti-heroes stand against the main heroes of the Book of Ezra. The opponents intervene with the imperial government to stall the efforts at rebuilding the temple.

Ezra 6 demonstrates that the author of the Book of Ezra has access to official documents in the archives of the Persian Empire. The Persian monarchs were obsessed with preserving continuity in their legal system. What one monarch decreed could not be annulled by any of his successors, or even by himself. So, when the Samaritans challenged the right of the Jews to rebuild their temple, the king Darius sent researchers into the archives and discovers the letter of his predecessor Cyrus authorizing the work. The dispute was settled legally, and the work of rebuilding the temple could continue.

The short Book of Ezra compresses a number of events spanning over a century. The exile lasted half a century, while the events of "the return from exile" took at least twice as long. Readers of the Book of Ezra may struggle to remember whether the events described are in the reign of Cyrus or Darius or Artaxerxes. Matters are complicated by the fact that imperial Persia had three rulers named Darius and two named Artaxerxes. In addition, the Book of Ezra seems to call the ruler Cambyses by the name Artaxerxes (Ezra 4:7–23). One should not conclude from this that the author of Ezra was ignorant of history. The history he described was his own, and he was a historian of events contemporary to himself. If Jews wanted to call Cambyses by the name Artaxerxes, they may have had some reason for doing so, of which we are unaware. They had a right to call their own rulers by any name they chose, as people do in every age. However, using more than one name, or using nicknames can prove to be confusing to others.

Thankfully, the Books of Haggai and Zechariah provide precise dating for the prophetic oracles which those two prophets received—six prophecies in the year 520 BC, one in 519 BC, and another in 517 BC, Such precise dating is rare in the prophetic literature generally, and in this case, assists the reconstruction of a timeline for the events in the Book of Ezra. Because of the testimony provided by those books, we know that nearly twenty years separate the events in chapter one of Ezra from those in chapter five. In 537 BC the temple treasures were returned to the land. Whereas, only in 520 BC did the Jewish people accelerate the rebuilding of the temple, and thus, bring it to completion.

Remember that the Ark of the Covenant was brought to Jerusalem in the reign of King David, but the temple to house the ark was not built until the reign of his son King Solomon. For many decades, the ark continued to reside in a tent, pitched within the city of Jerusalem, before the building of the First Temple. Similarly, the temple treasures returned to Jerusalem two decades before the building of the Second Temple.

What did the Jews do for twenty years when they returned to the Holy Land? Among other things, they waited for the word from God. Just as Solomon built only under divine command, so the returnees wanted to build only in response to God's directive, in God's time, not their own time. Those divine instructions finally arrived by means of Haggai and Zechariah.

First Prophecy of August/September 520 BC—*"Thus says the LORD of hosts: Consider how you have fared. Go up to the hills and bring wood and build the house, that I may take pleasure in it and that I may appear in my glory, says the LORD"* (Haggai 1:7–8). God directs the people to gather supplies and get started.

Second Prophecy of August/September 520 BC—*Then Haggai, the messenger of the LORD, spoke to the people with the LORD's message, "I am with you, says the LORD"* (Haggai 1:13). God reassures the people that He is with them.

Third Prophecy of August/September 520 BC—*"For thus says the LORD of hosts: Once again, in a little while, I will shake the heavens and the earth and the sea and the dry land; and I will shake all nations, so that the treasures of all nations shall come in, and I will fill this house with splendor, says the LORD of hosts. The silver is mine, and the gold is mine, says the LORD of hosts. The latter splendor of this house shall be greater than the former, says the LORD of hosts; and in this place I will give prosperity, says the LORD of host"'* (Haggai 2:6–9). God will prosper His people.

Fourth Prophecy of October/November 520 BC—*"Therefore say to them, Thus says the LORD of hosts: Return to me, says the LORD of hosts, and I will return to you, says the LORD of hosts"* (Zechariah 1:3). Repent, and turn to the Lord.

Fifth Prophecy of November/December 520 BC—*"Consider from this day onward, from the twenty-fourth day of the ninth month. Since the day that the foundation of the LORD's temple was laid, consider: Is the seed yet in the barn? Do the vine, the fig tree,* the pomegranate, and the olive tree still yield nothing? From this day on I will bless you* (Haggai 2:18–19). God will bless once again.

Sixth Prophecy of November/December 520 BC—*"Speak to Zerubbabel, governor of Judah, saying, I am about to shake the heavens and the earth, and to overthrow the throne of kingdoms; I am about to destroy the strength of the kingdoms of the nations, and overthrow the chariots and their riders; and the horses and their riders shall go down, every one by the sword of his fellow. On that day, says the LORD of hosts, I will take you, O Zerubbabel my servant, the son of Shealtiel, says the LORD, and make you like a signet ring; for I have chosen you, says the LORD of hosts"* (Haggai 2:21–23). God has the power to execute His plans.

Seventh Prophecy of January/February 519 BC—*"Therefore, thus says the LORD, I have returned to Jerusalem with compassion; my house shall be built in it, says the LORD of hosts, and the measuring line shall be stretched out over Jerusalem. Cry again, Thus says the LORD of hosts: My cities shall again overflow with prosperity, and the LORD will again comfort Zion and again choose Jerusalem"* (Zechariah 1:16–17). The temple will be rebuilt and God's people will prosper.

Eighth Prophecy of November/December 517 BC—*"Thus says the LORD of hosts, Render true judgments, show kindness and mercy each to his brother, do not oppress the widow, the fatherless, the sojourner, or the poor; and let none of you devise evil against his brother in your heart"* (Zechariah 7:9–10). Practice justice and mercy.

The prophecies to Haggai are very task-oriented: *build the house* (Haggai 1:8). The prophecies to Zechariah reconfirm that prophecy: *my house shall be built* (Zechariah 1:16). The Book of Zechariah is fourteen chapters long as compared to Haggai's two chapters. The considerably longer prophecies of Zechariah go on to recapitulate all the important concerns of the great and noble tradition of Israelite prophecy—true relationship to God, *"return to me"* (Zechariah 1:3), and just dealings with others *"Render true judgments, show kindness and mercy"* (Zechariah 7:9). The mystical visions of Zechariah rise well above the immediate concerns of the returnees, and claim a place among the most magnificent visions of the whole of biblical literature.

Two great things were happening in the Holy Land in the days of the return from exile. One of the greatest temples in the world was being rebuilt, and the two great prophets were speaking for Almighty God. From these post-exilic prophecies and the vision of Zechariah, the Book of Revelation will draw heavily for the images of the seven-branched candlestick (Zechariah 4:2; Revelation 1:12), the four colored horses (Zechariah 6:2–3; Revelation 6:2–8), and the measuring line (Zechariah 2:1; Revelation 21:15–17). The images that God gives to the Old Testament prophets reappear again in the New Testament.

1. Identify the resistance to rebuilding the temple. Ezra 4:1–5

2. In what language did people write the accusing letter? Ezra 4:7

3. In your own words, describe the content of the protest letter. Ezra 4:11–16

* Have you ever written a protest letter or editorial? What was your tone?

4. Explain the result of the accusatory letter to the king. Ezra 4:17–24

** Did you ever embark on a good project and have it thwarted by others?

5. Who came to the rescue? Ezra 5:1–2

6. Use a dictionary to define "prophet."

* Identify three prophets (those who speak for God) in our time.

7. Explain the drama in Ezra 5:3–5.

8. How did the re-builders of the temple identify themselves? Ezra 5:11–12

** How would you identify yourself to a non-Christian? Are you bold or shy?

9. What good news do they report? Ezra 5:13–16

10. What suggestion do they make to the king? Ezra 5:17

11. What did the king do and what did he find? Ezra 6:1–5

* How important is it to research and find out what was really said?

12. After his findings, explain the decree that Darius issued. Ezra 6:6–10

13. What would happen to those who interfered with the builders? Ezra 6:11–12

14. How did the people commence working on the temple? Ezra 6:13

15. Through what did the elders of the Jews prosper? Ezra 6:14

16. What feasts were celebrated? Ezra 6:17–22

17. With what emotion did the people celebrate? Ezra 6:16, 22

* What feasts of the liturgical year bring you the most joy?

18. Explain the prophecies of Hagai and Zechariah during this time.

Haggai 1:2–11
Haggai 1:13
Haggai 2:6–9
Zechariah 1:2–6
Haggai 2:10–19
Haggai 2:21–23
Zechariah 1:16–17
Zechariah 7:9–10

19. Would prophecy be fulfilled or abolished? Matthew 5:17-20

20. Compare Sirach 31:15 and Luke 6:31 with Zechariah 7:9–10 above.

CHAPTER 12

The Good Scribe
Ezra 7–10

Ezra went up from Babylonia.
He was a scribe skilled in the law of Moses
which the LORD the God of Israel had given;
and the king granted him all that he asked,
for the hand of the LORD his God was upon him.
Ezra 7:6

In chapter seven of the Book of Ezra, the scribe Ezra finally makes a belated appearance in his own book, which only contains ten chapters in all. In most biographical works, the subject appears from the very beginning to the very end. The absence of Ezra from the first two-thirds of the text indicates that this particular book is not a work of biography. Although Ezra is the most important figure, the author intended this as a work of history rather than biography. The Book of Ezra is the story of a people's return from exile, not merely the story of one specific man in particular.

Even with that disclaimer, the author and his community clearly held the person of Ezra in high esteem. The author provides Ezra's entire genealogy back to Aaron, the first high priest, so there would be no mistaking his priestly authority (Ezra 7:1–5). In the very next line, however, the author honors him as a scholar. *He was a scribe skilled in the law of Moses which the LORD the God of Israel had given* (Ezra 7:6). In Hebrew culture, not all priests were scribes, and not all scribes were priests. In fact, hardly any of the priests were scribes, though many of the scribes may have been priests. There were many priests, but few scribes. Among priests one was the highest, the high priest at any given time. Among scribes, none of them are higher than Ezra in any time.

What were the functions of a scribe? The first skill taught at scribe school was how to read. Very few people in ancient times could read. In ancient Egypt and Babylon, reading was a special job and skill. Not until the invention of the printing press were reading materials available to the general population, and then the goal of universal literacy became possible. Naturally, people of the book, like the Jews and Christians, foster literacy to make their sacred scriptures accessible to ordinary people. Nonetheless, illiteracy is still common, with one billion non-literate persons, fifteen years of age or older, in the world today. Two thirds of all non-literate adults are women. One half of all non-literate people live in India and China. A number of third world countries whose cultures are similar to those of biblical times have very high rates of illiteracy. But, Ezra the scribe was blessed to be able to read the biblical documents that had been handed down in his time.

The second skill taught to scribal students was the ability to write. All who write can read, but not all who read can write or type. Reading is a passive skill, while writing is an active skill. For a person to understand a foreign language is passive, to speak it is active. To read a text in one's own language is passive, to write it is active. Obviously, unless someone writes, no one else can read. The writer can become a copyist. Before there was photocopying or even printing, important documents had to be recopied, by hand, every few centuries. During the so-called Dark Ages, Benedictine monks recopied some of the literature of Latin antiquity over and over, so that they would survive for later generations. Other scribes were at work among the Jews and the Greeks, leaving a trail of manuscripts that modern scholars can follow in establishing the text of Scripture. Without the scribes and copyists, hardly anything would have survived.

The third skill taught to scribes was declamatory ability. To understand is one thing, to proclaim the truth to someone else is another matter. Most people would rather read to themselves than read publicly. Those who can and do read aloud perform a most valuable function, however, liberating the literature from the covers of the book out into the real world. The Bible was originally read this way—by one lector, to a group of people, large or small. In other words, the method of proclamation employed in the Liturgy of the Church today is exactly the way in which the Sacred Scriptures were intended to be presented to the faithful. Private reading is indispensable, but only when someone reads from the book to others does the full valence of the text become actualized. The book wants to be heard, not just seen. Ezra declaims the text of the Torah and in this way touches the hearts of the people.

The fourth skill, practiced by only great scribes, was the editing of texts. An author like Jeremiah, who was illiterate, dictated his prophecies to a scribe like Baruch, who put the words on paper. Baruch and others arranged the small scrolls into larger scrolls, until they reached the dimensions of the biblical books as they appear today. Around Ezra's time, much editing was done on the received Hebrew literature, and Ezra himself may have been the greatest of these editors. Editors usually prefer to remain anonymous, but ancient legend suggests the names of two men who edited the Bible as we have it—Onesimus, who may have edited the letters of Saint Paul, and Ezra, who may have edited the entire Torah himself.

The fifth skill of an ancient scribe was encyclopedic knowledge of the literature. Before the invention of writing, tribal societies had an oral historian, who committed to memory the accumulated knowledge of the community. After writing came along, readers with good memories took over this function of tribal historian. By New Testament times, the Jewish scribe had become someone to consult on questions of the interpretation of law. When King Herod wanted to know where the Messiah was to be born, he called in scribes, who were able to quote for him the prophetic passage about Bethlehem (Micah 5:2 in Matthew 2:3–6). Ezra, from his knowledge of the Torah, emphasized certain statutes to be enforced in the Jerusalem community, particularly the marriage law.

The Book of Ezra quotes several official Persian documents, some of them in the Aramaic language, which was the native tongue of many of the Jews, as well as one of the official administrative languages of the Persian Empire. There is every reason to believe that the biblical text incorporates actual court documents in their original languages. All of them are in Aramaic except the first, which appears in Hebrew (Ezra 1:1–4) and later in the original Aramaic (Ezra 6:1–5). The second letter presents itself half in Hebrew, half in Aramaic (Ezra 4:7–16), and may have been bilingual to begin with. Here is an itemization of these documents:

Letter of Cyrus (Ezra 1:2–4)
Letter of Samaritans to Artaxerxes (Ezra 4:7–16)
    the first half in Hebrew translation, the second in original Aramaic
Response of Artaxerxes to the Samaritans (Ezra 4:17–22)
Letter of the governor Tattenai to Darius (Ezra 5:6–17)
Response of Darius (Ezra 6:6–12)
    including archived Letter of Cyrus (Ezra 6:2–5)
Transit Letter of Artaxerxes to Ezra (Ezra 7:11–26)

The lists of participants in the first return (Ezra 2:1–70) and in the second return (Ezra 8:1–20) are also official documents, probably submitted by Sheshbazzar in the first case, and by Ezra himself in the second case, to the imperial court. The king would want to know when there was a large movement of his subjects, and in case one of the local satraps challenged the travelers, they would need to show the royal stamp on their passenger list. In effect, these documents were their passports for internal travel within the empire. The generally peaceful condition of the empire allowed Ezra's group to travel without military escort, for as Ezra himself admits, he was ashamed to ask for soldiers since he had declared to the king his total trust in God (Ezra 8:22).

As Tobit had done before in his book, Ezra speaks in the first person for part of his book (Ezra 7:27–9:15). Again, this seems to be an historical document, part of Ezra's own travel diary, covering both his departure from Persia and his subsequent arrival in Jerusalem. The intensely personal nature of this section allows a glimpse into Ezra's spirituality. He declares a fast before departing for the Holy Land (Ezra 8:21). And he rends his garments and pulls his hair when he discovers that some of those in the Holy Land had married foreign women (Ezra 9:3).

In deeper antiquity, intermarriage was not absolutely forbidden. The patriarch Judah married a non-Jewish woman, Tamar. Moses had married a Midianite woman. The Judahite Boaz had married the Moabite Ruth, a convert to the Hebrew people and God. King David married the widow of Uriah the Hittite, so Bathsheba was probably a Hittite woman. These marriages were so prominent that non-Jewish women are mentioned by name in the King's List found in chapter one of Matthew. Non-Jewish blood was intermingled with that of the House of David, the one divinely appointed dynasty, and the forebearers of Jesus Christ.

The problem of intermarriage was that it weakened religious observance, and became more acute when the people were struggling to survive against all the forces of history that were weighed against them during the exilic and post-exilic periods. God never insisted on DNA testing for membership in the people of God—if so, Ishmael would have had equal claim with Isaac.

The problem became more acute when a Hebrew man married a non-Hebrew woman, rather than the other way around. The mother bequeathed to her sons her language, her stories, and her culture. Frequently, the wife outlived her husband by many years, and her continuing influence would outweigh his, even if she were living with her in-laws. Moses himself seems not to have circumcised his sons immediately, waiting for his Midianite wife to embrace the faith first. Because there were so many domestic regulations that distinguished Jews from their neighbors—rules having to do with the preparation and serving of food, the cleaning of dishes, and bathing and menstrual issues—a non-Hebrew woman could hardly pass on to her daughters what she herself had not received from her own mother.

The rabbinic rule that tribal identity comes from the mother's side rather than the father's could well have originated during the exilic or post-exilic period. While the Israelites were on their own land, tribal identity was associated with the land, except in the case of Levites, who did not have their own portion on the land, but lived in priestly cities. After first the northerners, and then the Judahites had lost their affiliation with the land, they needed to have a rule of thumb. Otherwise, simple marriage between a man of Judah and a woman of Naphtali would have resulted in the tribal identity of their children being undetermined.

Genetically, a person is more closely related to the maternal side, because while the inter-nuclear DNA is derived from both parents, the extra-nuclear RNA comes entirely from the mother. When first cousins have mothers who are sisters, they share the same RNA as their common maternal grandmother. The Hebrews were not the only ancient people who understood this. The Latin language has a different word for maternal uncle *avunculus,* than for a paternal uncle *patruus.* A niece or nephew's relationship with one was considered very distinct from the relationship with the other.

Ezra becomes so distraught with the marriage problem that he is driven to extreme measures—he makes a comprehensive list of all the mixed marriages, and issues a blanket annulment, along with the expulsion of the children issuing from these marriages. As the husbands add their signatures to his declaration, the Book of Ezra ends. One is left to imagine whether the husbands actually did what they said they would do, or whether after dismissing the wives and children as promised they did not bring some of them home again. The author leaves much unsaid. Imagine what would happen in a Catholic parish if a pastor ordered all the men to dismiss their non-Catholic wives and disinherit their children. The bishop would certainly be called to intervene. In Ezra's case, some of the husbands would certainly have sought to go over his head to the imperial authorities. Perhaps the royal cupbearer Nehemiah himself would be called to intervene.

The Book of Ezra continues nicely into the Book of Nehemiah. In the Septuagint they are called First Ezra and Second Ezra. Two other ancient writings, a contemporary one called Third Ezra and a much later one called Fourth Ezra, are not included among the inspired writings. Those other documents wrap themselves in the cloak of Ezra in order to attract readership for themselves.

1. List some things that describe Ezra. Ezra 7:1–10

2. How did God favor Ezra? Ezra 7:6, 9

3. Summarize Artaxerxes' letter to Ezra in your own words. Ezra 7:11–20

4. What did Artaxerxes write to the treasurers? Ezra 7:21–24

5. What did the king recognize in Ezra? Ezra 7:25; Sirach 1:5

* Describe the wisest contemporary person you know.

6. How did Ezra respond to the king's decree? Ezra 7:27–28

** What virtue can be found in Ezra 7:28b? Do you possess this virtue?

7. What problem did Ezra identify in Ezra 8:15?

8. How did he attempt to remedy the situation? Ezra 8:16–20

9. What did Ezra do to obtain God's protection? Ezra 8:21–23

10. What can the Christian to do as a form of penance? CCC 1434, 1438

11. Find Ezra's practice in the Precepts of the Church. CCC 2042–2043

You shall attend Mass on Sundays and holy days and rest from servile labor.

* Which precept of the Church challenges you the most?

12. Explain what Ezra did after praying and fasting. Ezra 8:24–30

13. What did God do for Ezra and the returning exiles? Ezra 8:31

14. What problem is discussed in Ezra 9:1–2 and 2 Corinthians 6:14?

* Explain how the intermarriage problem could manifest itself today.

15. How did Ezra react to his discovery of this problem? Ezra 9:3–4

** List some practical ways to deal with unfaithfulness to God today.

16. Explain Ezra's prayer (Ezra 9:6–15) in your own words.

17. What does Ezra's prayer show? CCC 2585

18. How did Shecaniah propose solving the problem? Ezra 10:1–5

19. What did Ezra do that night? Ezra 10:6

20. What direction did Ezra give the people? Ezra 10:11

* Has God ever asked you to make a difficult change in your life? Explain.

Monthly Social Activity

This month, your small group will meet for coffee, tea, or a simple breakfast, lunch, or dessert in someone's home. Pray for this social event and for the host or hostess. Try, if at all possible, to attend.

The people of Israel often faced infidelity to God. Some people and nations in contemporary times also disregard and disobey God. Think of a contemporary problem and several practical ways to respond. Decide upon one of them. Share with your group.

Examples

A culture of death is emerging in our society. All life is a precious gift from God, from conception to natural death. Therefore, I could:
- ◆ *Pray for a woman facing an unexpected pregnancy.*
- ◆ *Pray in front of an abortion clinic and provide sidewalk counseling.*
- ◆ *Help a family with a special needs child.*
- ◆ *Visit a nursing home, or a homebound parishioner*

Pornography is an increasing problem in our society.
- ◆ *Move the computer to a common area of the home.*
- ◆ *Activate parental controls on all computers*
- ◆ *Fast and pray for those who are addicted to pornography*

CHAPTER 13

The Good Cupbearer
Nehemiah 1–6

"O LORD God of heaven, the great and terrible God who keeps covenant and merciful
love with those who love him and keep his commandments;
let your ear be attentive, and your eyes open, to hear the prayer of your servant,
which I now pray before you day and night for the sons of Israel your servants,
confessing the sins of the sons of Israel, which we have sinned against you.
Yes, I and my father's house have sinned."
Nehemiah 1:5–6

The Good cupbearer—Following the Book of Ezra, whose name means "help" or assistance," comes the Book of Nehemiah, whose name means, "My comfort is the Lord." Ezra's name is a prayer "Help!" while Nehemiah's name gives reassurance. These two giant figures of the return from exile have very different personalities, and different strategies, but they worked toward one and the same end, the reestablishment of Jewish life in the Holy Land. Ezra the scribe held an important position in the community, but Nehemiah out-ranked him. The position of cupbearer, which Nehemiah held, was the second-ranking position in the entire Persian Empire, after that of the king himself.

The role of cupbearer emerged in history in the courts of great kings. The cupbearer was also the official wine taster, who drank from the wine chosen for the king himself before serving it to the king. If the cupbearer fell dead, then the king would know that the wine was poisoned and would not drink from it himself. Because of this danger, and the importance of the cupbearer's role, the monarch rewarded such loyalty handsomely, because the life of the monarch depended on the loyalty of this servant. A poorly paid cupbearer might be tempted to poison the wine himself!

The cupbearer could never make a single mistake, even of the smallest kind. Greek art shows that the cups served at court were often wide-rimmed, to enhance the taste of the wine through oxidation. So the cupbearer had to have good balance. Spilling the wine or mead onto the lap of an oriental potentate was an unforgivable breach of etiquette, and the consequences would certainly have included impalement or crucifixion. So, the cupbearer literally took his life into his own hands every time he carried the royal cup to present to the king.

A cupbearer may occasionally have had musical duties as well. One and the same young man seems to be serving wine on the outside of a Greek bowl from Euaion, while playing flutes to the ruler on the inside of the bowl (Sully Branch of the Louvre, first floor, room 43, case 24). In those rare cases when the monarch himself was a musician, like King David, the cupbearer would also have had charge of the king's musical instrument.

The first cupbearer to appear in all of history was Sargon of Akkad in the twenty-third century BC. A Sumerian text called the "Sargon Legend" describes how, after a dream, Ur-Zababa, King of Kish, appointed Sargon, son of a gardener, as his cupbearer. It is hard to know from such an early period exactly what Sargon's duties as cupbearer were, and the legend itself only says that the king called him in to interpret one of his dreams. The king ordered the chief smith, and subsequently asked his neighboring king of Uruk to murder Sargon, but both times Sargon escaped. Eventually, Sargon became King of Kish himself and conquered the neighboring kingdoms to establish the first enduring empire in the Middle East. His offspring succeeded him on his throne to the sixth generation in a dynasty that lasted for two centuries. That was quite an achievement for a humble cupbearer, and lent promise and allure to the position for two millennia to come.

Cupbearers held an official position in the household of the Pharaohs of Egypt. The hieroglyphic sign shows a man down on one knee, holding a cup before his face, and represents the Coptic word *wdpw* rendered *butler* or *cupbearer* in Genesis 40:1. The butler apparently outranks his fellow royal officer, the baker, because he relates his dream first, before the baker. The cupbearer conveniently forgets that Joseph exists after the latter helped him regain his position, possibly because he felt threatened by Joseph's abilities. As events unfold, Joseph seems to put the cupbearer out of work, when he is given responsibility for administration of the entire land of Egypt. Although, Genesis does not put it in exactly those words, an Egyptian of that time would have thought that Joseph had become a super-cupbearer.

Although the Genesis account does not name the cupbearer who introduced Joseph to Pharaoh, other cupbearers appear by name in Egyptian texts. The cupbearer Tja-way has left a record of himself in four images:

1) A statue was found in the First Hall of the Temple of Mut in Karnak in 1858 and now is on display in the Egyptian Museum in Cairo.

2) A statue was discovered across the river at Deir el-Bahri and is now standing headless in the British Museum in London.

3) A relief stela was retrieved from a tomb in Sakkara, and is now housed in the Egyptian Museum in Cario.

4) From the same tomb as the latter antoerh, a relief stela was acquired in the early 1970s by the Museum of Fine Arts in Boston.

Only a very important figure would have left behind so many images. The Hebrew word for cupbearer in the Joseph story and elsewhere is *mashqeh* (Genesis 40:1), which literally means, "one who serves a drink." When the Queen of Sheba came to visit King Solomon in Jerusalem, she was overwhelmed by, among other things, the cupbearers (1 Kings 10:5), and their clothing (2 Chronicles 9:4). The chief cupbearer served the king himself, but would have found assistance from a whole team of fellow cupbearers to serve the king's guests at table.

When Sennacherib of Assyria captured Lachish, he sent the *Rabshakeh* (Isaiah 36:2), against King Hezekiah in Jerusalem. In Hebrew, the word *Rabshakeh* meant "the great cupbearer," but in the Assyrian language it means "the great prince." Since the context is clearly military here, and the cupbearer was a civilian, the Hebrew dictionaries now derive the term in Isaiah from the Assyrian usage.

When living in exile from their own homeland, Hebrew youths seem to have had the qualities needed to rise to the second tier of power. Joseph became administrator of the whole land of Egypt, equal to, if not supplanting entirely, the official cupbearer. King Esarhaddon of Assyria appointed the Nephtalite youth Ahikar as *cupbearer, keeper of the signet* (Tobit 1:22), from which position he was able to provide help to his uncle Tobit and the rest of his family. Daniel, Hananiah, Mishael, and Azariah assumed administrative positions in the Babylonian empire, and one of them, Mishael, acquires the Babylonian name Meshach, which loosely resembles the word for cupbearer. Nehemiah acquires the actual title under the reign of the Persian King Artaxerxes (Nehemiah 1:11). So, Hebrew youths at various points in history served in the highest positions in the royal courts of all the surrounding empires—Egypt, Assyrian, Babylonia, and Persia!

After the time of Ezra and Nehemiah, next door in Egypt, women began to till the role of cupbearer. In bilingual Ptolemaic inscriptions, the old hieroglyph for cupbearer translates the Greek word *kanephore* or basket-bearer, and old Greek religious term for a priestess who carried the basket during ritual processions. The Canopus Decrees of 238 BC mentions a woman named Menekrateia as a cup/basket-bearer, and the Rosetta Stone of 196 BC mentions a woman named Areia in that post. Apparently women could rise to high positions in the Egyptian royal court during the Ptolemaic period, because the sister of the king ruled co-equally with him, and appeared jointly with him on coinage and in inscriptions. Hence, the last member of the Ptolemaic dynasty to rule Egypt was Cleopatra VII, who initially had been co-ruler with her brother Ptolemy XIII.

Josephus relates how, in his final years, King Herod the Great had employed a cupbearer at his court. "There were certain eunuchs which the king had, and on account of their beauty was very fond of them, and the care of bringing him drink was entrusted to one of them, of bringing his supper to another, and of putting him to bed to a third, who almost managed the principal affairs of the government" (*Antiquities of the Jews*, XVI, viii, 1). An informer told the king that the king's son Archelaus had bribed three eunuchs, who were duly tortured to the very utmost, until they confessed. Needless to say, the king needed to find three more good servants after these were no longer trusted, or physically fit for service.

That incident from the Herodian court may lie behind some of the language Jesus uses with His disciples. When Jesus of Nazareth asks His disciples, *"Are you able to drink the chalice that I am to drink?"* (Matthew 20:22), and later at the Last Supper, bids them *"Drink of it all of you"* (Matthew 26:27), He makes Himself cupbearer, a servant to them, just as when He washes their feet. Jesus already appointed His disciples as cupbearers to Himself in their service to the lowly: *"And whoever gives to one of these little ones even a cup of cold water because he is a disciple, truly, I say to you, he shall not lose his reward"* (Matthew 10:42).

In all of these places the New Testament Greek uses the word *poterion,* which indicates a simple drinking cup, not a fancy vessel. The Latin Mass uses the word *calyx,* which gives rise to the English word "chalice." In the new translation of the Roman Missal, *calix* is usually rendered "chalice," as in the words of institution: "He took the chalice" and so forth. The word *cup* continues to appear some of the time, however, as in the second Memorial Acclamation: "When we eat this Bread and drink this cup, we proclaim your Death, O Lord, until you come again." That particular acclamation comes from the Last Supper narrative in Paul's First Letter to the Corinthians: *For as often as you eat this bread and drink the chalice, you proclaim the Lord's death until He comes* (1 Corinthians 11:26).

After the time of Christ, cupbearers continued to function in both pagan and Christian royal courts. In the kingdom of Visigothic Spain, one of the palatine officers was called the Count of the Cupbearers. In the Holy Roman Empire, the King of Bohemia held the rank of Arch-Cupbearer, only during the coronation service itself. Until the thirteenth century, a man with the title of Czesnik kept the wine cellar for kings of Poland and Lithuania, and the position became so important that it was absorbed as a title of the king himself since the fourteenth century.

The Christian liturgy resonates with some of the etiquette that belonged to the Christian courts of the East and West. The Extraordinary Minister of Holy Communion, in serving the Blood of Christ to faithful communicants, fulfills this dignity of Christian cupbearer in a very special way. The holy men Ahiqar and Nehemiah served the cup to secular kings, but in the Christian Liturgy the Minister of the Cup serves the King of Kings Himself to His kingly people: *But you are a chosen race, a royal priesthood, a holy nation, God's own people, that you may declare the wonderful deeds of him who called you out of darkness into his marvelous light* (1 Peter 2:9).

Returning from exile, Nehemiah the cupbearer, challenged and organized his people to rebuild the wall of Jerusalem. For a city without a wall could be easily invaded. Nehemiah had to overcome opposition from enemies and friends as well. But, God was with him. The city wall was rebuilt in less than two months, which so impressed Israel's enemies that they could see that God was with Israel. While Nehemiah organized the rebuilding of the wall, Ezra rebuilt the people's spirit, concentrating on restoring their spiritual health and fidelity to God's law. So, Ezra and Nehemiah made up a mighty team for God.

1. What bad news did Nehemiah learn? Nehemiah 1:1–3

2. How did Nehemiah react to the bad news? Nehemiah 1:4

3. Outline Nehemiah's prayer to God.

Nehemiah 1:5
Nehemiah 1:6
Nehemiah 1:7
Nehemiah 1:8–9
Nehemiah 1:10–11

4. Why were the people punished? Nehemiah 1:6–7

5. What is required for troubles to be alleviated? 2 Chronicles 6:24–25

* How can you pray for the troubles of your nation and work to change them?

6. Explain the drama in Nehemiah 2:1–3

7. What does Nehemiah ask of the king? Why does the king respond?

| Nehemiah 2:5, 7–8 |
| Nehemiah 2:8b |

8. Why were Sanballat and Tobiah displeased? Nehemiah 2:9–10

* Explain a plan to do something good for God that met with resistance?

9. With whom did Nehemiah share his plans? Nehemiah 2:11–12

10. When did Nehemiah inspect the damage to the walls? Nehemiah 2:13–16

11. What did Nehemiah suggest to his people? How did they respond?

| Nehemiah 2:17–18 |
| Nehemiah 2: 18b |

12. How did Nehemiah respond to the naysayers? Nehemiah 2:20

13. How should you explain your hopes and plans? James 4:13–15

* What project or enterprise would you ask God to bless right now?

14. How was the work of rebuilding organized? Nehemiah 3

15. What is unusual about Shallum's section of the wall? Nehemiah 3:12

16. What was devised against the Jews rebuilding the wall? Nehemiah 4:1–2, 7–8

17. How did they work and defend at the same time? Nehemiah 4:13, 16–23

18. What enabled Nehemiah to succeed? How did Nehemiah encourage the people?

Nehemiah 4:4–5, 9
Nehemiah 4:14

* Find someone to encourage this week, and then share with your small group.

19. Describe what happens in the following passages.

Nehemiah 5:1–5
Nehemiah 5:6–13
Nehemiah 5:14–19

20. Briefly explain the drama in these sections.

Nehemiah 6:1–14
Nehemiah 6:15–19

** Share an experience in which you completed something for the Lord.

CHAPTER 14

Reading the Torah
Nehemiah 7–10

And Nehemiah, who was the governor, and Ezra the priest and scribe,
and the Levites who taught the people said to all the people,
"This day is holy to the LORD your God; do not mourn or weep."
For all the people wept when they heard the words of the law.
Nehemiah 8:9

In Nehemiah chapter seven, the narration changes from first person to third person. The title of this book reads: *The words of Nehemiah, the son of Hacaliah* (Nehemiah 1:1), which accurately describes the first six and the last two chapters. For five chapters in the middle, however, someone other than Nehemiah seems to function as narrator, with Nehemiah mentioned three times in the third person (Nehemiah 8:9, 10:1 and 12:26). Much of the material in this section seems to be quoted from pre-existing documentation, as one sees so frequently in the Book of Ezra. In fact, the principal figure here is no longer Nehemiah the Cupbearer but rather Ezra the Scribe! Chapter Eight of the Book of Nehemiah belongs to Ezra.

First Reading—Suddenly in chapter eight of the Book of Nehemiah, the Scribe Ezra comes forward to read the Torah to the assembled people in Jerusalem. The survival of God's word in and of itself constituted the fulfillment of promise. Through His word, God continues to be present among his people. What Ezra did that day was a great Liturgy of the Word, like that of the Easter Vigil, which in the times of the early Church lasted all night. Usually the Bible is read in both synagogue and church in small segments, following various lectionary arrangements. Extremely rare are such occasions for longer readings in the Catholic liturgy.

A few highly motivated individuals have taken on the task of memorizing the entire Gospel according to Mark, and go around reciting the whole text in a single evening. At a remote rural location in America, one Catholic pastor reads the entire Sermon on the Mount to his parishioners in a single reading once a year. The Torah of Moses is much longer than the Gospel according to Mark, and even longer yet than the Sermon on the Mount. The Sermon on the Mount covers three chapters. The Gospel according to Mark lasts for sixteen chapters. Whereas, the Torah spreads out over one hundred eighty-seven chapters!

Ezra translated the Torah as he went. The Torah was in Hebrew, but the people likely spoke Aramaic. Until very recently it was the practice in the synagogue for the lector to read, first in Hebrew and then in Aramaic. The lector translated passages from the Torah verse-by-verse, but passages from the Prophets clustered in sets of three verses. Thus Ezra's reading of the Torah must have proceeded very slowly, double the time that it would have taken to read straight through.

Ezra had barely time to read just one book of the Torah, and that would probably have been the Book of Exodus, which contains the story of the Passover along with the giving of the commandments on Mount Sinai. The people would be more likely to weep for joy over that book than over the other four, though they all have their moments. Of all the books, Exodus encapsulates most the essence of what it means to be the People of God. If the Old Testament held but a single book, it would have to be Exodus. A mandatory reading for the Easter Vigil each year is the account of the crossing of the Red Sea (Exodus 14:15–31).

Second Reading—On the following day, Ezra met with the heads of families and the Levitical priests and showed them the passages regarding the Feast of Booths (Exodus 34:18–26, Leviticus 23:33–43 and Deuteronomy 16:13–17). One passage of special significance was the instruction of Moses for a reading of the Torah to be given during the festival of Booths every seventh year (Deuteronomy 31:10–11). Ezra's actions are in compliance with Deuteronomic legislation, and clearly indicate that he was using that book from the Torah.

Ezra held his first reading on the first day of Tishri, the seventh month of the old calendar, which had New Year in spring. Later, when the New Year transferred to fall, the seventh month became the first. So the first day of Tishri, when Ezra read the first time, became Jewish New Year, a two-day celebration from dawn on the first day until sundown on the second day of the month.

Feasts of Tishri (September–October)

1 Tishri—New Year's Day
2 Tishri—New Year's Second Day
15 Tishri—First Day of Booths
16 Tishri—Second Day of Booths
17 Tishri—Third Day of Booths
18 Tishri—Fourth Day of Booths
19 Tishri—Fifth Day of Booths
20 Tishri—Sixth Day of Booths
21 Tishri—Seventh Day of Booths
22 Tishri—Great Festival Day of Booths

Complete Reading—The festival of Booths lasts for eight days, from the fifteenth to the twenty-second day of the month of Tishri (seventh month in the old calendar, first month in the new calendar). Ezra read the Torah every day during that octave. (He must have had a very good set of lungs!) Counting the reading on the first day of the month, Ezra did public reading of the Torah for fifty-four hours. If his Aramaic translations were abbreviated, he could have read substantially the same text, as we know it, during that time.

Quotations from Ezra's edition of the Torah appear in the books of Ezra (Ezra 7:6, 10, 14) and of Nehemiah (Nehemiah 8:14–15), but none of those verses appear anywhere in the received text. That indicates that further editing of the Torah continued after Ezra's time, and the data suggests a shortening rather than a lengthening of the text, perhaps a collation of different manuscript traditions.

Illumination of Conscience—The reading of the Torah was a great examination of conscience for the Jews, some of whom may have broken the commandments knowingly and others of whom acted in ignorance. For all it provided enhancement of the faculty of conscience. Thus the reading of the law is followed in chapter nine by a great act of public confession, a foreshadowing of the Sacrament of Penance. Their ritual included readings from the Law along with admissions of guilt.

Chapter nine of the Book of Nehemiah connects to the narrative in chapter ten of the Book of Ezra. The relationship between the two narratives is very close, without being parallel like those in the synoptic gospels. One needs to read Ezra and Nehemiah globally, since the narratives proceed not in a fully linear manner.

Firm Purpose of Amendment—In Nehemiah 10, the people sign a pact and recommit themselves to observing some of the commandments, which they had found themselves guilty of breaking. At the head of the promise appear the names of eighty-four individuals, divided into three groups (priests, Levites and leaders of the people). The first of the names is Nehemiah. Ezra's name does not appear here.

The first provision of the pact is: *We will not give our daughters to the peoples of the land or take their daughters for our sons* (Nehemiah 10:30). The practice of intermarriage with pagans must stop. There were other provisions made for the keeping of sabbath of days, the sabbath of years, a temple tax of a third of a shekel each year, and a tithe for the support of the priests. The latter taxes were suspended while the temple was in a state of ruin, but after it's rebuilding the inherent obligation to contribute to its support becomes effective again.

Meet the Chronicler—The problem of intermarriage is a principal theme of four historical books of the Bible: 1 and 2 Chronicles, Ezra and Nehemiah. For that reason, along with reasons of style, scholars give the name "the Chronicler" to the author of those books. Could the Chronicler have been Nehemiah himself, later in life editing his autobiography into the quilt work of a larger work? As a member of the imperial household, he would have had access to the archives, from which the Chronicler draws material in his writings.

Could the Chronicler have been Ezra the Scribe? An editor like the Chronicler would need to have scribal skills in order to do his work. An original author can dictate to a secretary, but the collation of manuscripts requires for the editor to possess personal literacy as well as excellent organizational skills.

Was the Chronicler a third person, neither Ezra nor Nehemiah? Certainly those two men were so busy that they hardly had time left over to edit four historical books covering the whole history of Israel from David down to their own time, a total spanning over six hundred years. A fourth possibility presents itself—that the Chronicler was not a single person, but a committee comprising Ezra and other scribes, along with Nehemiah and other dignitaries of the imperial court. This may comprise the same group that gathered and grouped the books of the Torah and Prophets into their final ensemble. That was a huge undertaking, and was more likely the work of many than of only one.

More than one manuscript tradition existed already. The Book of the Prophet Jeremiah still exists to this day in two very different editions, one represented in the Hebrew and the other in the Greek of the Septuagint. The Chroniclers do not seem to have addressed that problem. Perhaps they recognized both versions as coming from Jeremiah himself.

Why did the Chroniclers wish to retell the whole history of the Israelite monarchy in 1 and 2 Chronicles, when 1 and 2 Kings had already quite thoroughly covered the material? They dealt with the same basic facts, but their theological interpretation of the sacred history took a different tack. The two books of Kings document the authenticity of the Davidic claim to rule over Israel, and the catastrophic consequences of failing to follow in David's line. The two books of Chronicles reveal the ongoing subversive influence of the Canaanite false religion in Israelite life. The latter set the stage for the issues treated in the books of Ezra and Nehemiah, where the residual influence of paganism constitutes the principal challenge confronting the returnees to the holy land.

Nehemiah overcame opposition from enemies and his own people to rebuild the wall protecting Jerusalem. Once Nehemiah had completed the city wall, Ezra sought to rebuild the spiritual health and spirit of the people. Spiritual health can be restored with a good examination of conscience and repentance. Reading God's Word aloud and reflecting on the commandments provides a great aid for personal and communal reflection. While the people want to weep for their sins, there is great joy in repentance and reconciling sinners to God. Confession and a firm purpose of amendment allow the returning exiles to get right with God. The same pattern is true throughout all of history.

Those who return from a far country, a place of sin and separation from God, can find peace and joy once again. Reflecting on the commandments of God, examining one's conscience, repenting of sin, and making a firm purpose of amendment can bring great joy today, just as it did in the time of Ezra and Nehemiah. Just as the exiles returned to Jerusalem with Nehemiah in 444 BC, another group of Jews would return to their homeland nineteen hundred years later. In 1948, following the horrors of World War II and the Holocaust that destroyed the lives and hopes of so many of the Jews, many survivors returned to Israel to rebuild a nation. Similarly, those who are exiled from God by sin and rebellion, can return home to Him, through reflection, repentance, and the Sacrament of Reconciliation.

1. Who was placed in charge of Jerusalem and why? Nehemiah 7:1–3

2. What happened in Nehemiah 7:5–7?

3. How large was the whole assembly? Nehemiah 7:66–68

4. How did people show their gratitude to God? Nehemiah 7:70–72

* In what specific, practical ways can you show your gratitude to God?

5. Describe the events in Nehemiah 8:1–8.

6. How did the people respond to hearing God's law read? Nehemiah 8:9b

7. Who gave what advice to the people? Nehemiah 8:9–12

8. Identify the activity described in Nehemiah 8:13.

* How and when do you *study the words of the law* (Nehemiah 8:13)?

9. Explain the Feast of Booths from these references.

Leviticus 23:33–42
Deuteronomy 16:13–16
Ezra 3:4
Nehemiah 8:13–18

10. What problem recurs among God's people?

Nehemiah 9:2
Nehemiah 10:30
2 Corinthians 6:14

** What problems can arise when a believer and an unbeliever marry?

11. How does Ezra begin his prayer to God? Nehemiah 9:6–8

12. What event does Ezra recall? Nehemiah 9:9–15

13. How did the people behave?

Nehemiah 9:16–17
Nehemiah 9:18
Nehemiah 9:26
Nehemiah 9:28
Nehemiah 9:29

14. How did God behave?

Nehemiah 9:17b
Nehemiah 9:19–20
Nehemiah 9:21–25
Nehemiah 9:26–31

15. How does God act? Nehemiah 9:33

16. Define the word "covenant." Nehemiah 9:38

17. What did the people promise God that they would do? Nehemiah 10:29

18. What activities do the people promise to forego? Nehemiah 10:30–31

19. Find one word to describe the activity in Nehemiah 10:35–38.

20. What final promise is made to God? Nehemiah 10:39b

* How can you care for *your* temple of the Holy Spirit? 1 Corinthians 6:19–20

** List several ways you can show greater respect in the house of God.

CHAPTER 15

Dedicating the Wall
Nehemiah 11–13

*And the people blessed all the men
who willingly offered to live in Jerusalem.*
Nehemiah 11:2

Structure of the Book of Nehemiah

Nehemiah 1:1–7:3	Nehemiah gives autobiographical information.
Nehemiah 7:4–12:26	Nehemiah is named three times, in the third person.
Nehemiah 12:27–13:30	Autobiographical data is provided by Nehemiah.

From the very first verse of his book, Nehemiah narrates in first person (usually using the singular "I" but sometimes the plural "we"). In chapter seven that style is interrupted for a third-person description, but in the middle of chapter twelve the first-person narrative resumes. In the first section, Nehemiah tells how he went to Jerusalem to oversee the rebuilding of the city wall, and in the third section, he tells how the wall was blessed. So the wall is the big framing theme of this book. Clearly, for the cupbearer himself, his unique contribution to the cause of the return from exile was the rebuilding and rededication of the walls of the city.

The Original Wall—An ancient city had to protect itself from marauders and invaders, and had to offer a place of sanctuary for traders, shepherds and pilgrims. The builders of city walls became heroes to the local inhabitants: among his other accomplishments, legendary King Gilgamesh built the walls of Uruk. The Jebusites built a walled city called Jebus or Salem (double name Jebus-Salem apparently contracted to become Jerusalem). Their rulers were priest-kings in the line of Melchizedek (Psalm 110:4), who had offered unbloody sacrifice at the time of Abraham (Genesis 14:18). So Jerusalem was a holy city already before it became the capital of Israel. Thus the walls were sacred, too.

David conquered Jerusalem without a destructive siege, thus leaving the Jebusite walls intact. Those walls continued in use, but David expanded the city *from the Millo inward* (2 Samuel 5:9), and Solomon refurbished the walls on the eastern side adjacent to the temple mount. The author of Psalm 48 regards these walls themselves as matter of legend: *Walk about Zion, go round about her, number her towers, consider well her ramparts, go through her citadels; that you may tell the next generation that this is God, our God for ever and ever. He will be our guide for ever* (Psalm 48:12–14).

The Broad Wall of Hezekiah—Under threat from the Assyrians in 725 BC, King Hezekiah built a massive new perimeter wall, eight yards thick. Isaiah congratulated the king with these words: *and you saw that the breaches of the city of David were many, and you collected the waters of the lower pool, and you counted the houses of Jerusalem, and you broke down the houses to fortify the wall* (Isaiah 22:9–10).

A century and a half later, the Babylonians came and tore down Jerusalem's Broad Wall: *And all the army of the Chaldeans, who were with the captain of the guard, broke down the walls around Jerusalem* (2 Kings 25:10). Throughout the period of the exile and even after, the city site remained vulnerable to plunder and pillage: *Why then have you broken down its walls, so that all who pass along the way pluck its fruit* (Psalm 80:12).

The Wall of Nehemiah—Cyrus the Persian liberated the Jews and allowed them to return to the Holy Land, but Jerusalem remained a city without defenses. That was fine with the Persians, because after they conquered Egypt there was no longer any threat of foreign invasion from that direction. A century later, the Persian hold on Egypt weakened, and then they authorized Nehemiah to rebuild the walls. This meant that they trusted the Jews to be loyal subjects and not to use the wall as a means of shutting them out. It also meant that they felt they could use the Jewish city as part of a line of defense against the Egyptians.

Nehemiah and his fellow leaders ordered the foundations of the wall of Hezekiah to be used as the base for their own rebuilding: *and they restored Jerusalem as far as the Broad Wall* (Nehemiah 3:8). Hezekiah had torn down houses to obtain materials for his wall, and Nehemiah reused many of those same stones himself. Employing materials twice recycled, the Wall of Nehemiah was not one of the wonders of the ancient world, but it possessed deep meaning for Jews. Rebuilding the walls put some closure on the long period of exile. It was one thing to return in person, and another to rebuild the temple, but the third big phase was to restore the walls. Until the wall went back up, Jerusalem remained a city despoiled and disgraced. Nehemiah clothed the city again, removing her shame.

The Wall of Herod—Marc Antony and Augustus Caesar regarded King Herod the Great as a trusted client, and permitted him to endow the Holy Land with numerous fortresses including Masada, Machaerus and the Herodion (his fortified tomb). When he rebuilt the Second Temple, Herod shored up the sides of the temple mount with gigantic ashlar stones characteristic of Herodian construction. In so doing, he greatly reinforced the defense capabilities of the eastern wall of Jerusalem. The pilgrims to Jerusalem marveled about these walls: *And as he came out of the temple, one of his disciples said to him, "Look, Teacher, what wonderful stones and what wonderful buildings!"* (Mark 13:1). Jesus wept when he foresaw their destruction (Luke 19:41).

Jesus knew all the walls of the historical Jerusalem, both those which had come before him and those which would come thereafter. He did not weep for the walls of the Jebusites or the Herodians, or the walls of the Romans or the Turks. He wept for the walls of

Nehemiah, the humblest of all the walls but those invested with the most devotion, the most love, the most sanctity. Jesus knew how pure were the motives of Nehemiah in building walls for the holy city, and so those were the walls most beautiful in his sight.

The Wall of Herod Agrippa—The city of Jerusalem apparently experienced tremendous expansion under the Pax Romana, and at the middle of the first century King Herod Agrippa expanded the area of the city westwards, incorporating new residential districts to meet the expanded local population as well as the huge number of pilgrims arriving from all over the world for the three Jewish high holydays of Passover, Pentecost and Booths. The site of the crucifixion, which had been outside the city in Jesus' time, fell within the city limits at this time. The building of the new wall may have given the zealots overconfidence and helped propel them toward the disastrous revolt against Roman rule. The Judean revolt shook the empire and helped bring down the Julio-Claudian dynasty that had ruled for a century. At the end of the war, however, Rome was still standing while Jerusalem was destroyed. The Romans had no trouble demolishing the Wall of Herod Agrippa, but being practical people they mostly left in place the gigantic ashlar stonework of Herod the Great along the eastern wall of the city.

The Wall of Revelation—After the destruction of the historic city of Jerusalem, the author of the Book of Revelation had a great vision of a New Jerusalem: *Then I saw a new heaven and a new earth; for the first heaven and the first earth had passed away, and the sea was no more. And I saw the holy city, new Jerusalem, coming down out of heaven from God, prepared as a bride adorned for her husband* (Revelation 21:1–2). The apocalyptic Jerusalem will have no need of defensive walls, but the prophecy assigns to her glorious walls anyway: *It had a great, high wall, with twelve gates, and at the gates twelve angels, and on the gates the names of the twelve tribes of the sons of Israel were inscribed; on the east three gates, on the north three gates, on the south three gates, and on the west three gates. And the wall of the city had twelve foundations, and on them the twelve names of the twelve apostles of the Lamb* (Revelation 21:12–14).

The Wall of Hadrian—A second Jewish Revolt took place sixty years after the first, led by Bar-Kochba. As a consequence, the emperor Hadrian expelled all Jews from the Holy Land, and rebuilt Jerusalem along the lines of a pagan Roman colony, under the name Aelia Capitolina. Hadrian set up pagan temples on both Jewish and Christian sacred sites, and enclosed the new city in a small perimeter wall. Later, the Christian Emperor Constantine demolished the pagan temples in Jerusalem and built Christian basilicas, but Hadrian's walls remained in use throughout the Byzantine and early Islamic period.

The Wall of Suleiman—During the Crusader period, the old Roman walls suffered greatly both from wartime siege and an occasional earthquake. To correct this situation, the Ottoman Turkish Sultan Suleiman the Magnificent in AD 1538 built the walls, which still today surround the Old City of Jerusalem. The Old City of Jerusalem along with its walls was inscribed on the UNESCO World Heritage Site list in 1981. The walls are nearly three miles in length and boast forty-three surveillance towers and eleven gates, seven of which are open.

Open Gates in the Old City of Jerusalem

English Name	Hebrew Name	Arabic Name
Damascus Gate	Shaar Shechem	Bab al-Amud (Gate of the Pillar)
Herod's Gate	Shaar ha-Frihim	Bab az-Zahri (Florists' Gate)
Stephen's Gate	Shaar ha-Aryot	Bab Sittina Mariam (Our Lady Mary's Gate)
Dung Gate	Shaar ha-Ashpot	Bab al-Maghariba (Moroccans' Gate)
Zion Gate	Shaar Zion	Bab an-Nabi Dawud (Prophet David's Gate)
Jaffa Gate	Shaar Yafo	Bal al-Khalil (Hebron Gate)
New Gate	Shaar Hadith	Al-Bab al-Jadid (New Gate)

Of these currently open gates, the Damascus Gate stands on the same location as the northern-facing gate of Hadrian's wall, because the Roman gate can still be seen on a lower level, along with a mile-marker which is the source of the Arabic name for the gate. Other gates must be in the same general location as the ancient gates, because they face towards the four directions of the compass, towards the same ancient cities with which the people of Jerusalem have done business at every phase of her history.

Currently bricked up is the very ancient eastern-facing double portal, which Herod called the Susa Gate, but which has mostly been called Golden or Beautiful Gate (the Horaia Pyle, Shaar Yafe, al-Bab al-Jalil). Outside this gate Saint Peter performed an act of healing: *And a man lame from birth was being carried, whom they laid daily at that gate of the temple which is called Beautiful to ask alms of those who entered the temple* (Acts 3:2). In Jewish tradition, when the Messiah came he would enter the city through that gate. Islamic authorities took the Jewish tradition seriously and bricked the gate up to keep the Messiah out.

The walls of a holy city exist not to keep people out, but to define a sacred space to which people are invited to come. The holy wall is therefore significant mainly for its gates: *Lift up your heads, O gates! and be lifted up, O ancient doors! that the King of glory may come in* (Psalm 24:7/9). Jesus never calls himself a wall, but he does call himself the point of entry: *"Truly, truly, I say to you, I am the door of the sheep. . . . I am the door; if any one enters by me, he will be saved, and will go in and out and find pasture"* (John 10:7, 9).

1. What did the Jewish people do in Nehemiah 11:1–3?

* Recall a similar event that took place after World War II.

2. Who was the overseer of the city of Jerusalem? Nehemiah 11:9

3. How many Levites lived in the holy city? Nehemiah 11:18

4. Who were the gatekeepers of the holy city? Nehemiah 11:19

5. Who was in charge of the singers in the house of God? Nehemiah 11:17, 22–24

** How important is music ministry in your parish? How does music help worship?

6. Where did the remainder of the people live? Nehemiah 11:25–36

7. Who was in charge of the songs of thanksgiving? Nehemiah 12:1–8

8. Who stood opposite them in service? Nehemiah 12:9–11

9. How were people arranged and ordered? Nehemiah 12:12, 22

* Who is the head of your household?

** Who is the head of your parish?

*** Who is the head of your diocese? Do you regularly pray for these people?

10. What job did the Levites have? Nehemiah 12:24

11. What responsibility did Mattaniah and Obadiah have? Nehemiah 12:25

12. How was the dedication of the wall celebrated?

Nehemiah 12:27–30
Nehemiah 12:31–37
Nehemiah 12:38–43

13. List the towers and gates in the procession. Nehemiah 12:38–39

Towers	Gates

14. Explain the importance of singing hymns and psalms of praise to God.

Nehemiah 12:45–47
CCC 2588
CCC 2641

15. Describe the emotions of the men, women, and children. Nehemiah 12:43

16. Why were Moabites and Ammonites excluded? Nehemiah 13:1–3

17. Explain the drama in Nehemiah 13:4–14.

18. Compare the following verses.

Exodus 20:8–11
Nehemiah 13:15–22
CCC 2172

19. What practice is condemned in these verses?

Nehemiah 13:23–27
2 Corinthians 6:14

20. What did Nehemiah do and what did he ask of God? Nehemiah 13:14, 30–31

* What good things would you like people to remember about you?

CHAPTER 16

Defending the Faith
1 Maccabees 1
2 Maccabees 1–5

*But many in Israel stood firm and were resolved in their hearts
not to eat unclean food.*
1 Maccabees 1:62

The collapse of the Persian Empire marked the true beginning of Western Civilization. Until then, the center of power had always been in the East, but now the cultural center shifted westwards. For some time, Greek things have fascinated Middle Eastern people. Ideas went ahead of Alexander the Great to prepare the way before him. Greek ideals were modern. Eastern ways were considered old-fashioned.

The books of the Maccabees graphically chronicle the clash between these two ideologies, the ancient Semitic practices of the East, and the more nuanced Greek ways of the West. It was the opening salvo in a clash of cultures that continues to this day. Whatever today is liberal or rational claims a Greek origin; whatever is conservative or religious traces itself back to the Semites. How to reconcile these two aspects of our heritage is a challenge that we share with the Maccabees, who confronted the problem for the very first time.

In the Second Century BC, a whole literature grew up around the Maccabean revolt, the story of one family—the Maccabees who stood firm in their faith, and were willing to fight for Judaism against false religious influences. Four volumes survive to this day, two of them contained within the traditional Christian (Catholic and Orthodox) Bible. A fifth book existed, but now is lost. These writings fill a void in our knowledge of the experience of the people of God through the four centuries between the time of Nehemiah and that of Jesus. Much changed during that time, with the fall of Persia, the rise of Greece, the decline of the Greek kingdoms and the rise of Rome. The Jews, both in the Holy Land and in the diaspora, were buffeted by these changes and had to struggle against the forces of history to retain their identity. Their story is worth remembering; their books are worth reading.

Jews and Persians—Several books of the Hebrew Bible document the special alliance that existed between the Jewish people and the Persians. The term *messiah* "anointed one" in Isaiah 44:28–45:1 describes the first Persian emperor Cyrus, who brought down the Babylonian captors of the Jewish people. Apparently these good feelings continued down through the reign of the subsequent emperors. Jews, such as Nehemiah, rose to the highest levels in the court. Perhaps the Jews appreciated the Persians at first just because they were not Babylonian, but their friendship endured so long that there must have been mutual respect. The Magi, following a star, would come from Persia to the Holy Land looking for the newborn king.

To connect their far-flung empire, the largest in history to that day, the Persians built the first network of roads. Darius I built a great highway, the Royal Road, stretching 1,677 miles from the administrative capital of Susa westward to the Aegean port city of Sardis. Pedestrians could walk the distance in ninety days; riders would take seven days in a relay system called *Chapar Khaneh*. Like the other people in the empire, the Jews could travel these roads for trade, communication and travel. As a result, a large Jewish community formed in Sardis at the far end of the highway. The ancient name of that city is Sepharad, and from that comes the historical designation of Mediterranean Jews as Sephardic Jews.

Jews in the Holy Land never actually achieved political independence under the Persians. In essence, the Jews were treated as loyal subjects. Throughout the Persian period, Jews thrived and their numbers grew throughout the known world. They benefited from the cosmopolitan outlook and opportunities provided them.

Perhaps one additional factor creating a common cause between Jews and Persians was that the latter were not polytheists in the usual sense of the word. They did not worship many gods; their *deva* were devils, not divinities. The Iranians were dualists, like the Slavs; they believed in two forces at conflict in the world, a force for good and a force for evil. Occasionally biblical authors mirror such terminology, when contrasting light and darkness. Jewish theologians could easily identify their own one, true God as the force for good in the universe, while not elevating any opponent to the same degree.

Jews and Greeks—The arrival of the Greeks disturbed the situation. The generals of Alexander the Great divided his conquests between them, putting up boundaries where the Persians had none. The general Ptolemy ruled Egypt from Alexandria and founded the Ptolemaic dynasty; the general Seleukos ruled Syria from Antioch and founded the Seleucid dynasty. Nearly every king of Egypt was called Ptolemy, and nearly every king of Syria was called Antiochus (thirteen of them). They were distinguished from each other by their second name—two of those named Antiochus had the same second name, Antiochus IV Epiphanes (215–164 BC) and Antiochus XI Epiphanes, who died in 92 BC without ruling. *Epiphanes* meaning "Shining Upon" is one of the titles of the Greek supreme god Zeus. The name Epiphanes was also borne by the last king of Commagene, Gaius Julius Antiochus IV Epiphanes.

Boundaries now appeared where previously the Persians had none. Customs agents appeared on roadways, slowing down the flow of commerce. The Judeans found themselves once again a border people, caught between two larger kingdoms, as they had been back in the days of the monarchy. For about a century, they were under the rule of Egypt, but then the Syrians brought them into their dominion.

Egyptian customs were closer to Jewish usage than Greek customs. The Hebrews had lived in Egypt for a number of generations, and understood Egyptian ways, even if they were foreign; but Greeks were novel, and the vigor and conviction of Greek ideals seemed at odds with traditional Judaism. For example, the Greeks burned their dead in funeral pyres and placed the ashes in urns, because they did not believe in an afterlife. The Egyptians and Jews, on the other hand, preserved the bodies of their deceased, and buried them for the sake of eternal life.

The Common Background of Greek and Hebrew Civilizations by Cyrus Gordon maintains that things in the Hebrew Bible often parallel aspects of Greek culture. Many of his examples belong not to the classical Greek period, however, but to the Minoan and Mycenaean civilizations that flourished before Homer. Back in the days of Moses, proto-Greeks may have shared common Mediterranean culture with the Semites, and the "sea peoples" and Philistines of the coastal plain may have been Hellenic, but that took place many years before, and times had changed. If Gordon is right, then the Greeks and Jews tragically failed to recognize each other as heirs of a common heritage.

In the days of the Maccabees, the Seleucid monarchs of Syria functioned not like Greek tyrants, aristocrats, or demagogues, but like oriental potentates. Though they promoted Greek ways, their governance had little in common with traditions of Greek politics. The Seleucids already felt the growing influence of another power from further west, the Romans. Antiochus Epiphanes had been a hostage in Rome (1 Maccabees 1:10). He made war against Rome and suffered a crushing defeat, but Rome was not yet ready to absorb Syria into their empire, and so a massive fine was imposed instead. Epiphanes came down hard on the Jews from a rational fear that so long as they maintained separate customs they could be recruited as subversive agents within the Seleucid kingdom. One who sits fearfully on the seat of power constitutes the greatest potential threat to truth and justice.

Entering the Sanctuary—Epiphanes was not the first or the last pagan conqueror to enter the sanctuary of the temple in Jerusalem (1 Maccabees 1:21). Only the high priest was allowed to enter the holy of holies, and only once a year. But, Alexander had entered anyway, and later Ptolemy the Great also would do so. This act of entering was sacrilegious, but war gives opportunities to generals that no one can claim in times of peace. More gravely, Epiphanes seized the sacred objects of the temple as booty, and then instituted pagan worship in the temple. Jews called this action of Epiphanes "the abomination of abominations."

In the ancient world, religion and nationality intertwined. The Hebrew God commanded the lives of the Hebrew people and ruled their land, just as the false gods seemed to control the lives of other nations. Epiphanes wanted the Jews to accept the gods of Greece, and in this way to abandon any claim to independence.

For the Jews, however, during the five long centuries that transpired since the fall of the last Davidic king, their religion had become more important to them even than their own politics. Greeks and Romans had long come to consider their gods as myths, convenient for giving authority to the state, but otherwise irrelevant to daily life. During the same period, Jews had gone the other direction, so that what God did for each and every individual Jew (and vice-versa) was paramount.

Attack on the Torah—The word *Torah* in Hebrew means "teaching" both in general and the teaching of Moses in particular. The five books of Moses outrank the rest of the Hebrew Bible because they contain the teachings of Moses. A portion of those teachings comprise divine positive law given on Mount Sinai (the Exodus Code), as well as legislation seemingly crafted by Moses to meet the emerging needs of the Hebrew people in the desert—the Deuteronomic Code.

The Syrians seemed to know, or soon discovered, that for many Jews the five books of Moses were more important than the temple and its rituals. No temple is mentioned in the Torah, and the Jews got along perfectly well for centuries before Solomon built the first temple, and even after Nebuchadnezzar destroyed it. Even though the Jews were enjoying the Second Temple Period after the rebuilding, and the temple was a vivid symbol and rallying point for Judaism, the heart of the religion is exposed in the books of the Torah, the Prophets and the Writings, some of which still remained to be written.

Greek culture was based on the authority of a few prominent authors—poets like Homer or Sappho, philosophers like Plato or Aristotle, historians like Thucydides or Herodotus, mathematicians and scientists like Euclid or Archimedes. Their discoveries laid the groundwork, whether cultural, conceptual, political or economic, for the Greek cosmos. When a Greek orator wanted to wrap himself in the flag of Greek culture, he would quote one of the established authors, and that was a rhetorical flourish meant to bolster the force, if not the logic, of his argument. The practitioners of Greek logic criticized this technique, calling it the fallacy of appeal to authority. While nothing can be proven absolutely by quoting an author, such a written statement may be admissible as a fact of note in courts of law.

The Greeks who ruled Syria knew the Torah's importance to the Jewish people, and their desecration in burning the Torah was meant as an act of cultural genocide. If the Jews had lost the Torah, eventually they would have ceased to be Jews. Epiphanes wanted to separate the believers from their Bibles, and in that way to destroy their faith. His burning of the books reminds one of how the King of Judah had destroyed the first edition of the Book of Jeremiah the Prophet: *"As Jehudi read three or four columns, the king would cut them off with a penknife and throw them into the fire in the brazier, until the entire scroll was consumed"* (Jeremiah 36:23).

That king did not hate the Jewish people, but he does not seem to have had any love for the prophets, or at least Jeremiah, in particular. Presumably the king did not destroy God's word habitually or as a matter of public policy. What one Jewish king did personally once, out of spite, Epiphanes proclaimed as the law of his land. He did not hate literature, even sacred literature; he was simply trying to cut off the people's identity by lobotomizing them culturally. If they had found meaning in a comic book, he would have set out just as systematically to destroy every copy of comics that he could find. Epiphanes epitomizes all the fanatics of all time who burned books as their way of harming people.

The Relationship between First and Second Maccabees—Of the four extant volumes of Maccabean literature, First and Second Maccabees stand as the most important. They do not follow one another sequentially as First Samuel leads to Second Samuel, First Kings to Second Kings, and First Chronicles to Second Chronicles. Rather, they overlap and expand upon one another. What the author of First Maccabees treats summarily in his first chapter, Second Maccabees expatiates leisurely for five chapters.

Scholars consider First Maccabees to have been composed in the Hebrew language, though only the Greek translation survives. The original title was *Sarbeth Sarbanael*, which could be translated "The Book of the Dynasty of the Prince." That makes it seem to be a work of political propaganda to support the Hasmonean Dynasty that ruled in the Holy Land later in the century.

Second Maccabees also survives only in Greek and declares itself to be based upon another, now lost work: *"all this, which has been set forth by Jason of Cyrene in five volumes, we shall attempt to condense into a single book"* (2 Maccabees 2:23). Thanks to Jason, who has a Greek name and comes from a Greek city in Libya, we learn, in greater detail, the personalities and issues that led to the Maccabean revolt. Second Maccabees begins by preserving two letters, which the Jews of the Holy Land sent to Jews in Egypt. The point of view of Second Maccabees seems to be located in the diaspora, while that of First Maccabees is in the Holy Land itself.

Further details of the causes of revolt may be found in the writings of Flavius Josephus, in the twelfth and thirteenth books of his work entitled *Antiquities of the Jews*. Among other things he reproduces two letters authored by Epiphanes, seeming to indicate that at an early period he was not yet an archenemy of the Jews. The relationship between them soured over time, as such things sadly happen.

The beginning of First Maccabees and Second Maccabees sets the stage for the drama of those who stand firm in faith, under epochs of great oppression. Throughout the history of the world, God's people have faced times of trouble and periods of persecution. Some believers are weak in their faith and cowardly. Others are courageous and stand firm in their faith, despite oppressive circumstances. While studying the Maccabees, reflect on how strong a faith is required to stand firm and remain faithful to God in times of persecution.

Reflect on situations in contemporary society in which Christians may be called upon to stand firm in their faith. In a secular, relativistic culture, believers must be prepared to stand up for God and His principles and precepts. Standing firm in faith can lead to persecution and even martyrdom. Think of ways in which religious freedom is compromised in various cultures today. Imagine ways in which you might be called upon to stand up and defend the precepts of your faith in an increasingly ungodly culture.

1. How were some of the people of Israel misled? 1 Maccabees 1:11–15

2. What can you learn about Antiochus Epiphanes?

1 Maccabees 1:10
1 Maccabees 1:16–19
1 Maccabees 1:20–23
1 Maccabees 1:24
1 Maccabees 1:29–32
1 Maccabees 1:33–37

3. How did some of the Jews respond?

1 Maccabees 1:11–15
1 Maccabees 1:25–28
1 Maccabees 1:38–40

4. What did the king forbid? 1 Maccabees 1:41–49

5. How was the Torah desecrated? 1 Maccabees 1:56–57

6. What happened with respect to circumcision? 1 Maccabees 1:60–61

7. What happened to those Jews who did not forsake the Law?

1 Maccabees 1:53
1 Maccabees 1:62–63

8. To whom, from whom, and when is the letter in 2 Maccabees 1:1, 7 addressed?

9. What do the Jerusalem Jews ask the Jews in Egypt to do? 2 Maccabees 1:2–9

10. What did God do? 2 Maccabees 1:11–17

11. What did Nehemiah and the priests do? 2 Maccabees 1:18–23

12. For what did the people pray? 2 Maccabees 1:24–29

13. What had Jeremiah done? 2 Maccabees 2:1–12

14. List the main characters and tell the story of Maccabees. 2 Maccabees 2:19–22

15. Why were the holy Laws kept in peacetime? 2 Maccabees 3:1–3

* How can you promote faithfulness to God's Law and Catholic teaching?

16. Describe the drama in 2 Maccabees 3:4–14, the people's response and result.

2 Maccabees 3:4–14
2 Maccabees 3:14–22
2 Maccabees 3:22–30
2 Maccabees 3:31–34
2 Maccabees 3:35–40

17. Explain some of the main ideas in 2 Maccabees 4.

2 Maccabees 4:1–6
2 Maccabees 4:7–17
2 Maccabees 4:18–22
2 Maccabees 4:23–29
2 Maccabees 4:30–38
2 Maccabees 4:39–50

* List some ways in which wickedness and treachery appear today.

18. What did Jason do? 2 Maccabees 5:1–10

19. Who were these people and what did they do?

| 2 Maccabees 5:15–16 |
| 2 Maccabees 5:17–20 |
| 2 Maccabees 5:21–23 |
| 2 Maccabees 5:24–26 |

20. What did Judas Maccabeus and his friends do? 2 Maccabees 5:27

* How could you prepare yourself and your children to be courageous for the Lord?

** Do you think you could see religious persecution in your lifetime? Explain.

Martyrdom
1 Maccabees 2
2 Maccabees 6-7

So he died in his integrity, putting his whole trust in the Lord.
2 Maccabees 7:40

In the Greek language, *martyr* means "a witness." The supreme witness is Jesus Christ, who by shedding every drop of His blood testified to His love of the Father, and all the Father's children. Christian martyrs associate themselves with the witness of Jesus, and become witnesses in both life and death to their love of the One who is the source of all life. Jesus said that His followers would have to pick up their cross daily—the cross being an instrument of capital punishment—signifying that each day they should be ready if called upon to give their lives as He did.

By contrast, the Hebrew Bible did not highlight the concept of martyrdom, for it preceded the life and witness of Jesus. For Moses and the prophets, death was a punishment, and abundant life a reward. Many commandments of the Mosaic covenant had death as a penalty, while life was among the blessings of obedience. How the good God could allow a righteous man to suffer an inglorious death posed a pressing problem for the Hebrew mind.

The Maccabees introduced martyrdom as a major theme of Judaism practically for the first time, and in that way helped set the stage for the New Testament. Although the martyrs of the Maccabean revolt gave their lives for the old covenant, their means of expressing their absolute faith in God aligns them much more closely to the new covenant. Like the Holy Innocents, the little babes of Bethlehem, who were slaughtered as substitutes for the Baby Jesus, the Maccabees are more than forerunners to Christ; they actually participate already in the ethos of Christianity. The books of the Maccabees work equally well either as an epilogue to the Old Testament or as a prologue to the New Testament.

Martyrdom for what?—A person can witness for anything, bad or good. In modern times, some gave their lives for the sake of fascism, or communism. Even though their cause was flawed, they still paid the ultimate price for it. All martyrs pay the ultimate price, but the value of their sacrifice depends on the worthiness of the cause for which they stood. So the sacrifice of the Maccabees needs to be evaluated on the basis of what they valued more than life itself. Did their end justify the high price they paid? From our vantage point some twenty-two hundred years later, can we gain from what they gave?

The true martyr sacrifices his life for the truth of God's will. Martyrdom witnesses to God and to God's truth, for which there can be no response. Each believer must testify to the moral truth, which the Church faithfully teaches. Discipleship comes with a cost. Standing up for God's ways can cost friends, reputation, and advancement. Each disciple enters into that witness that the martyrs gave most completely for God with their very lives. Each person created in God's image and likeness is called to sacrifice in some significant way for Him. Some witness for God with their manner of living the truth of God's word, others witness by relinquishing their very lives for God, in the ultimate sacrifice—martyrdom.

Martyrs for the Law of Circumcision—In Jewish jurisprudence, circumcision holds a more fundamental place than the rest of the Mosaic Law. God made a covenant of circumcision with Abraham, subsequent to his initial covenant of faith, and so Abraham was circumcised himself along with his sons and servants. Consequently, this practice belongs to all the physical descendants of Abraham, including the Jews, Midianites, and Arabs. For those who dwell in the desert, where scant water makes good hygiene difficult, the removal of the foreskin seems to have the beneficial effect of preventing infections and cancers, thus adding to the male lifespan.

Antiochus Epiphanes pressured the Jews not to circumcise their children. Greeks regarded any amputation as a form of mutilation. In Greek philosophy, each individual man reflects the ideal of the perfect man, and no Greek man would voluntarily compromise his own perfection in any way. Greek feelings on the subject were not unique, of course—nobody likes to be cut. Judaeo-Christian legal interpretation sees self-mutilation as a grave offense against the fifth commandment: *You shall not kill* (Exodus 20:13). Jewish custom did not countenance the removal of any body part other than the foreskin, and in every other way, they were just as careful to keep body and soul together as the Greeks were.

In another way, however, Greeks and Hebrews differed greatly—in the realm of modesty. In cultic games, such as the Olympics, Greek athletes performed naked, because they saw the power and grace of their bodies as divine gifts. By Roman times it became customary to portray gods as naked and humans as clothed, but for the Greeks, nudity in life as well as in art was a sign of high humanity. Jews and other desert peoples covered themselves scrupulously to protect against the ultraviolet radiation of the sun, and for modesty. They were horrified by displays of nudity. When circumcised Jews wanted to participate in athletic activities in the Greek gymnasium (*gymnos* means "naked") they would undergo painful surgery to restore the appearance of a foreskin. If circumcision was painful, re-circumcision was far more so. Medical science was primitive in those days, and anesthesia did not yet exist. In submitting to such pain, the Hellenizing Jews showed that they valued the athletic club far more than their membership in the People of God.

Strict Jews naturally considered that surgical alteration a total surrender of Jewish values to the pervasive Greek ways. They defended circumcision not for its own sake, but as a symbol of their loyalty to the covenant. In that very spirit of loyalty to Jewish practice, Saint Joseph and the Blessed Mother offered their Son to the rite of circumcision on the eighth day after His birth. The traditional Roman Calendar has the feast of the Circumcision of Our Lord on the Octave of Christmas, the first day of

January. While in the new Roman Calendar, this feast now announces the Solemnity of Mary the Mother of God, the Gospel for that day still uses the passage describing the circumcision of Our Lord.

When the Savior submitted himself to the law of circumcision, His humanity and divinity were joined in an unbreakable bond of covenant, by which salvation is made possible for others. The faithfulness of the Jews, to the law of circumcision prepared the way for Christ's sharing in that covenant bond, and through Christ everyone who is baptized is baptized into Christ. When He was circumcised, Jesus for the first time shed His blood, one drop of which would have been sufficient to save the whole world, as Saint Thomas Aquinas said:

Me immundum munda tuo sanguine Cuius una stilla salvum facere Totum mundum quit ab omni scelere.	Clean my unclean self by your blood, Of which one drop could save All the world of every sin. From the hymn "Adoro te devote."

Had God the Father willed it to be so, the circumcision of Jesus could have been the saving act of cosmic salvation. Apparently, however, Jesus did not want to give only a little of His blood. Since many martyrs would give their last drop for Him, Jesus would not be outdone in generosity. His circumcision, however, was at least the first step in the Way of the Cross.

Martyrs for the Kosher Law—Every nation has its own dietary preferences and unique taboos. Americans avoid eating horse, rabbit or dog. Europeans eat horse and rabbit, but not dog. Native Americans never ate horses, because they did not have any; some tribes ate dog, while others did not. It was hardly unusual that the Jews shun pork, for example, because many of the desert dwellers had the same rule. Among the Jews, however, dietary laws rose to a level of prominence higher than in any other nation, except perhaps the Brahman caste of Hindus. The justification for kosher jurisprudence is simply the divine positive law, the Revelation of God, and no other nutritional or hygienic intent, even though those benefits were received.

Jewish kosher law is a reminder of the original commandment: *"But of the tree of the knowledge of good and evil you shall not eat, for in the day that you eat of it you shall die"* (Genesis 2:17). The breaking of that one command made necessary all other kinds of law. Though Saint Peter and the apostolic Council of Jerusalem would later abrogate application of kosher law, Church tradition is not without its own similar laws. The practice of abstaining from eating meat on Fridays, in remembrance of Our Lord's Passion and death, connects our sacrifices to those of Christ. As God, Christ created everything and nothing to Him was unclean, but as a Jewish man, Jesus observed the kosher laws that He himself had given.

Christians who follow the Crucified One identify with all people who have suffered for their religious conscience. Many people use the word conscience today as an excuse not to follow divine or Church law, but the properly formed conscience may bind us far more than it looses. Before submitting themselves to martyrdom, however, the good Catholic should make a good confession and consult the confessor. No one should march into danger unaccompanied by the power of the Holy Spirit, sacraments, and the good counsel of a spiritual director. Martyrdom could be an occasion of sin if one were tempted to deny Christ rather than die for Him, and who can presume in advance that one would not be weak and cowardly at such a time? Can we courageously accept martyrdom for Christ and forgive the one killing us for Christ? If not, we have no business putting ourselves in harm's way. Until then, admire the martyrs from afar, and pray for more courage.

Uncircumcised Christians who eat sausage shamelessly can read about the Maccabees and ask themselves why those people had to die to avoid doing what would later become commonplace. That would be missing the point, however. It was never just about pork or foreskins, but about doing the will of God: *"Blessed rather are those who hear the word of God and keep it"* (Luke 11:28). Those Christians may yet find themselves called to pay the ultimate price for what others would consider something of little value; many Christians have paid, and many more may yet be asked to do so. Should such a time arrive for any of us, may we prove as courageous and faithful as the Maccabees, who foreshadowed the Passion of the Christ, as well as future Christian martyrs.

Martyrs Compared—The different works of Maccabean literature highlight several different personal tales of heroism:

— The first book tells of the elderly zealot Mattathias, who kills a Jew who is about to offer sacrifice on a pagan altar (1 Maccabees 2:23–24).
— The second book of Maccabees tells of the elderly scribe Eleazar, who spits out force-fed pork, and so welcomes his death (2 Maccabees 6:18–31).
— An unnamed mother witnesses the martyrdom of all seven of her sons rather than disobeying God by eating pork (2 Maccabees 7).

First Maccabees emphasizes how some resisted violently, but Second Maccabees tells how others practiced civil disobedience. First Maccabees would applaud Saint Peter for cutting off the ear of Malchus, the slave of the high priest (John 18:10–11), while Second Maccabees would praise him for stretching out his hands, so that another could gird him and carry him where he would not wish to go (John 21:18). First Maccabees is more of a political tract, and Second Maccabees more of a spiritual one. First Maccabees is a gospel for the Zealots of New Testament times, while Second Maccabees shows us martyrs who resemble those who would be willing to forfeit their lives for Christ.

One incident from Second Maccabees uncannily parallels an incident from the life of a Christian martyr of the second century. The men in charge of Eleazar *privately urged him to bring meat of his own providing proper for him to use, and pretend that he was eating the flesh of the sacrificial meal which had been commanded by the king* (2 Maccabees 6:21). Similarly, the Roman judge who presided over the trial of Bishop Polycarp of Smyrna around AD 166, gave him the option of pretending to worship the emperor. But Polycarp replied: "For eighty-six years I have served Jesus Christ and He has never abandoned me. How could I curse my blessed King and Savior?" In both cases, Eleazar and Saint Polycarp, the elderly martyrs refused to save their own lives by pretending to denounce their faith. If they had chosen to do so, they would have been giving bad example to other believers, especially the young. Their consciences would not countenance such cowardice.

The martyred mother of Maccabees prefigures a number of martyred mothers in Christian history, including notably the mothers, Saint Perpetua and Saint Felicity of Carthage. Saint Felicity was with child when she was condemned to death, and the law did not allow pregnant women to be sent to the arena, but she gave birth and went almost immediately to her death. These mothers consigned their children to the care of others as they stood by their faith in Christ, and their faith and courage is the equal of the stamina shown by the mother in Maccabees.

Feast of the Maccabees—Calendars of the old Roman and Eastern Churches held many feasts honoring Old Testament saints: Ezekiel (April 10), Jeremiah (May 1), Isaiah (May 9 and July 6), Job (May 10), Elisha (June 14), Maccabee (August 1), Elijah (July 30), Joel (July 13), Abel (July 30), Moses (September 4), Abraham (October 9), Obadiah (November 19), Nahum (December 1) and Zephaniah (December 3). No one would assert that those dates correspond to either the death or the life of the saints in question. Perhaps for that reason, modern Church calendars exclude them, but they do retain feasts for those who lived right up to the time of the Messiah: John the Baptist (June 24 and August 29), Joachim and Ann, grandparents of Jesus (July 26), Zachary and Elizabeth, parents of John the Baptist (November 5) and the Holy Innocents (December 28).

The old Roman calendar calls the first day of August the feast of "the seven holy Maccabee martyrs." Calling the seven holy sons of the holy mother "Maccabees" is a little imprecise, for strictly speaking that term refers to the five sons of the zealot Mattathias. The liturgy certainly is entitled to bestow the spiritual title of Maccabee on the martyred brothers. In that sense may we all be worthy of the title Maccabee.

May the brotherly crown of your martyrs, O Lord, give us joy,
and offer increase of strength to our faith,
and console us through many helps.

(Proper Collect for the Feast of the Maccabee Brothers)

---

1. Who are the members of Mattathias' family? 1 Maccabees 2:1–5

2. List some atrocities or blasphemies that Mattathias saw.

1 Maccabees 2:6–7
1 Maccabees 2:8-9a
1 Maccabees 2:9b
1 Maccabees 2:10–12

3. What did Mattathias and his sons do? 1 Maccabees 2:14

4. How do Catholics mourn over sin today? CCC 1431

* What penitential practices do you regularly observe?

5. How did the king's officers try to persuade Mattathias? 1 Maccabees 2:15–18

6. How did Mattathias respond? 1 Maccabees 2:19–22

1 Maccabees 2:19–22
1 Maccabees 2:23–24
1 Maccabees 2:25–26
1 Maccabees 2:27–28

7. Describe another approach to faithfulness. 1 Maccabees 2:29–38

8. How did Mattathias react to that peaceful resistance? 1 Maccabees 2:39–41

* When are you inclined to be a fighter for the good, and when a peacemaker?

9. Explain the activity in 1 Maccabees 2:42–48.

10. Explain some of the last words of Mattathias to his sons. 1 Maccabees 2:49–51

* What would you tell your loved ones, if you knew your end was approaching?

11. Identify some of the traits of the heroes of Israel.

1 Maccabees 2:52	
1 Maccabees 2:53–54	
1 Maccabees 2:55–57	
1 Maccabees 2:58–60	

12. What advice does Mattathias give in 1 Maccabees 2:61–64?

13. List some final instructions.

1 Maccabees 2:65
1 Maccabees 2:66
1 Maccabees 2:67
1 Maccabees 2:68

* Israel mourned for Mattathias. Recall some Christians who were greatly mourned.

** What can you do to pray for your deceased loved ones? CCC 1471, 1479

14. Describe some atrocities and the reason for such calamities.

2 Maccabees 6:1–6
2 Maccabees 6:7–11
2 Maccabees 6:12–17

15. Explain the drama involving Eleazar.

2 Maccabees 6:18–20	
2 Maccabees 6:21–22	
2 Maccabees 6:23–28	
2 Maccabees 6:29–31	

16. How does the Catholic Church view Christian witness and martyrdom?

CCC 2471	
CCC 2472	
CCC 2473	
CCC 2474	

* Research and share the life of a contemporary martyr.

** In what specific ways have you been called to witness to God and to His truth?

17. Write the sentiments of the seven brothers facing martyrdom.

2 Maccabees 7:1–6
2 Maccabees 7:1–9
2 Maccabees 7:10–12
2 Maccabees 7:13–14
2 Maccabees 7:15–17
2 Maccabees 7:18–19
2 Maccabees 7:30–40

18. What did the mother say to her youngest son? 2 Maccabees 7:27–29

19. What spiritual truth did the mother reveal? CCC 296, 297, 298

20. What hope do the Maccabean martyrs share with us? CCC 992

* What does the resurrection of the body mean to you?

Monthly Social Activity

This month, your small group will meet for coffee, tea, or a simple breakfast, lunch, or dessert in someone's home. Pray for this social event and for the host or hostess. Try, if at all possible, to attend.

A martyr is a witness to the truth, and makes the supreme sacrifice for God. Share about some ways in which you have been called to witness to the truth at some personal cost.

Examples

◆ *Recently at a shower, my family members were joking about different kinds of artificial contraception. The room got very quiet when I mentioned the benefits gained by following the Church's teaching with respect to Natural Family Planning.*

◆ *Someone we care for very much announced that he would be celebrating a same-sex commitment ceremony, and invited us to attend the "so-called wedding." We declined in such a way that we tried to share the truth in charity.*

◆ *A young unmarried couple announced that they were planning on moving in together to save money. They thought it would be good to get to know one another before deciding to marry and asked me what I thought. I had a chance to explain God's plan to them, even though they weren't really expecting me to say anything.*

CHAPTER 18

Judas Maccabeus
1 Maccabees 3
2 Maccabees 8–9

"It is not on the size of the army that victory in battle depends,
but strength comes from Heaven.
They come against us in great pride and lawlessness to destroy us
and our wives and our children, and to despoil us;
but we fight for our lives and our laws.
He himself will crush them before us; as for you do not be afraid of them."
1 Maccabees 3:19–22

Popular uprisings generate leaders, who determine the outcome. A weak or bad leader can preempt and corrupt a worthy cause; only responsible leaders make real progress possible. The Maccabean Revolt proved successful in large part because it gave power to a series of noble men. Mattathias was blessed to have several courageous warriors among his sons, and the greatest was Judas. Though not of the family and lineage of David, he possessed a warrior's heart like that of the founder of the Israelite royal house. Any nation with a military commander like Judas could be rightly proud. Largely because of the battlefield successes of Judas and his brothers, the Jewish people managed successfully to bridge a transition from one imperial system to another. Upon arrival, the Romans found the Jews a proud and independent people, both abiding and ruling in their own land.

The Name Maccabee—The Hebrew term *Maqqebeth* was translated into Greek as *Makkabaio*, and into Latin as *Maccabaeus*, and into English as *Maccabee*. Occasionally the Latin spelling will appear alongside with the English. The Maccabean movement was fortunate to claim a distinctive battle name that never appears anywhere else in the long history of the Jewish people.

Maccabee is not a proper name, but a nickname given to Judas, son of Mattathias. The word comes from the Hebrew noun *maqqebeth* meaning "hammer" (1 Kings 6:7, Isaiah 44:12, Jeremiah 10:4), which in turn comes from the Hebrew root *naqab* meaning "to perforate," or "to designate." Although a hammer can be used as a weapon, it is not a proper weapon of war but an instrument of peace, used in building, in this case rebuilding. Judas Maccabaeus was a hammer used to refasten the Jews to their traditional religious ways.

The Maccabees were a reform movement within Judaism, as well as a military movement against the Greeks. Their true enemy was not only the Greeks, but rather Jews who had abandoned their religious practices to become militant Hellenists. Antiochus Epiphanes had local agents, apostate Jews who wished to obliterate their historical religion, so that they could better assimilate into the dominant culture. Their goal was to destroy, while the goal of the Maccabees was to build. So, the Maccabees became a hammer of building, not a mallet for demolition.

Division of Powers—On his deathbed, Mattathias bestowed civilian rule on his eldest son Simon, but military rule on his second son Judas (1 Maccabees 2:65–66). Neither of these sons claimed the title of king. They were to be known as Simon, the man of wise counsel (1 Maccabees 2:65), and Judas Maccabeus, the mighty warrior and commander of the army (1 Maccabees 2:66). Their functions were equivalent to governor and general.

Mattathias displayed great wisdom in distributing the governmental functions between his two sons. Simon held the higher position, as a father (1 Maccabees 2:65), and took care of the peacetime needs of the civilian people—the women, children, elderly, and infirm. Their wellbeing was critical to the success of the movement, because the fighting men needed to know that their families were being cared for in their absence, which left the morale of Judas and his fighters high.

Clearly the two brothers, Simon and Judas were on the same page, without sibling rivalry between them. Their cooperation with each other upheld the honor of their father's cause, and preserved their common patrimony of Jewish activism. Interestingly, their "patron saints," after whom they were named, were the full brothers Simon and Judah, legitimate sons of Jacob and his first wife Leah.

Later, Jesus would tell the parable of the prodigal son and his elder brother, and how they divided the patrimony between them. The shock value of that parable was very great for the original, Jewish audience, because of the high importance attached to the commandment to honor one's father and mother. Maintaining the patrimony, both material and spiritual, comprised a principal component of the respect, which was due to parents, who labored for their whole lives long to be able to leave something more to their children. Sill in our day, Jewish families place a high value on responsible management of inherited wealth.

The wealth that Mattathias left to his own sons was not merely a material estate, but a spiritual patrimony as well. Thus, when these brothers cooperated with each other, they kept alive their father's vision. If they had turned away, their father would have become a footnote to history. If he could not have even convinced his own sons of the importance of Jewish fidelity and activism, he would have left no legacy at all. Because they kept to his ways, they boosted the contribution that he made as a turning point in the historical place of his people.

Judas was successful in his initial military encounter, defeating the commander Seron at the battle of Beth-horon. This surprising rout caught the attention of the Syrian king, who sent forty thousand infantry and seven thousand cavalry to the Holy Land, intending genocide of the Jewish people. The Syrian invaders did not know what kind of a threat Judas' guerrilla forces could be to their conventional army. They were also totally unaware of the power of God.

Dynasty of the Maccabees

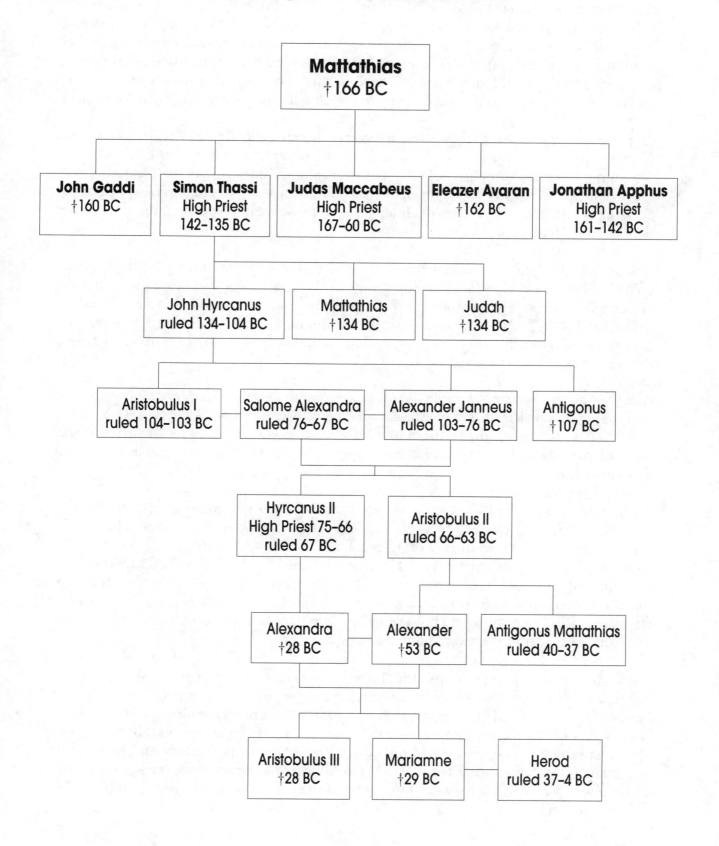

Had the Syrians been going out to meet the Egyptians, Persians or Romans in battle, their cavalry would have faced other cavalry, and their infantry would have faced other infantry. The Syrians, however, were an occupying power and they needed to defend held positions against mobile guerrilla forces. Cavalry and infantry demonstrate limited usefulness in such situations. The overwhelming force of the Syrians counted only in conventional battlefield situations; elsewhere, this was actually a disadvantage. They had too much of the wrong kind of army to match what Judas was putting into the field.

Again and again down through history conventional generals have rediscovered this simple truth—how hard it is to keep an army of occupation at the top of their game. The duties of occupation are police duties, not military ones. Judas the Maccabee was one of the first in history to see this truth and capitalize upon it. He practically invented guerrilla warfare, in which the advantage goes to those with fewer encumbrances rather than to those with more.

Religious and military historians have equally failed to give the Maccabees their proper credit. In both cases, the fact that the Books of the Maccabees were excluded from the Hebrew Bible probably accounts for the underestimation of what the Maccabees did for the history of the Jewish nation and for the history of warfare. They reinvented warfare to reaffirm religion. They were willing to fight and, if necessary, to die in order to defend the way of life God had given them.

Creating an Army from Scratch—Armies do not materialize out of nowhere. Great nations perpetuate a tradition of military readiness, discipline and experience. Otherwise, when danger threatens, the state could need years to come up to speed. By then it might be too late to defend the land, and ensure the victory. Swift defense is just as important as swift offense.

The Jewish people had no armies of any kind between the collapse of Jerusalem in 587 BC to the time of the Maccabees in 166 BC, a period of 420 years. The arts of war changed a great deal during that time, from the heavy infantry of the Babylonians to the light infantry of the Greeks. The first challenge facing Judas the Maccabee was to train and equip a force capable of meeting the forces of the Seleucid Kingdom. He may have been able to draw upon the skills of individuals who had served in the Greek style armies of Egypt or Syria, but even so he had to create an army from scratch. This was Judas Maccabeus' great achievement.

Once they had capable troops, the Jews had several advantages. First, they were fighting on their own soil. Second, their fighters were loyal to the commander and believed in the cause. Third, many of their opponents were mercenaries; some doubted the policies of Antiochus Epiphanes, while some of their home regions suffered under the same policies. The Jews could only capitalize on their motivation and home land advantage, however, with a truly capable and inspiring commander. The name of the commander was itself fortunate—a country named Judah (Judea) had a commander named Judah (Judas).

The name Judah or Judas—To the fourth of his sons, Jacob gave the name Judah, which means "praiseworthiness." The name came to belong to all the descendants of Judah, known collectively as the Tribe of Judah. The portion of the Holy Land given to that tribe, in the south around Hebron, acquired the name Judah or Judea. The people residing in Judea were called Judahites or Judeans. After most of the other Hebrew tribes disappeared, at the time of the exile, the whole Israelite people came to be called Jews. And, their religion was called Judaic or Jewish. In the Hebrew language, however, the same name Judah properly describes the founder and members of the tribe, the land and the religion of the tribe.

It is not unusual that Mattathias gave the name Judas to the second of his sons, because the name seems to have become very popular in the period of the return from exile. Six men from at least three different tribes bear the name Judah in the Books of Ezra and Nehemiah, and these are the only men with that name (besides Jacob's son) in the pages of the Hebrew Bible:

1) Judah, a man whose offspring helped rebuild the temple (Ezra 3:9)
2) A Levite who took a foreign wife (Ezra 10:23)
3) A Benjaminite administrator of Jerusalem (Nehemiah 11:9)
4) A Levite in charge of the songs of thanksgiving (Nehemiah 12:8)
5) A prince of the tribe of Judah at the dedication of the wall (Nehemiah 12:34)
6) Judah, a musical priest (Nehemiah 12:36).

The name Judas retained its popularity in the times of the New Testament, where as many as seven men share that name. In the English language, some of these are called Jude and some Judas, but all of them are called in the Latin *Judas*, in the Greek *Ioudas*, and in the Hebrew *Jehudah*:

1) Judas Iscariot, the betrayer of Jesus (Matthew 10:4)
2) One of the brethren of Jesus (Matthew 13:55, Mark 6:3)
3) The brother of James and letter-writer (Luke 6:16, Jude 1:1)
4) Jude Thaddeus or Judas (not Iscariot), (John 14:22)
5) Judas the Galilean rebel (Acts 5:37)
6) Judas who lived on Straight Street, and housed Saul in Damascus (Acts 9:11)
7) Judas called Barsabbas, companion of Silas (Acts 15:22, 27).

The greatest Judah in the Hebrew Bible was the son of Jacob. The greatest Judas in the New Testament was the apostle called Thaddeus, also known as Saint Jude Thaddeus. Judas the Maccabee takes his place alongside the other two, as the third greatest man ever to give honor to that name. The three of them exonerate the name, from the shame with which Judas Iscariot, the betrayer, besmirched it.

Handel's Oratorio—Over the course of his last two decades, George Frideric Handel wrote fifteen oratorios based on figures from the Bible—Esther in 1732, Deborah, and Athalia in 1733, Saul, and Israel in Egypt in 1739, Messiah in 1742, Samson in 1743,

Joseph and His Brethren in 1744, Belshazzar in 1745, Judas Maccabaeus in 1747, Joshua, and Alexander Balus in 1748, Susanna, and Solomon in 1749, and Jephtha in 1752. Of these compositions, Messiah is overwhelmingly regarded as Handel's masterpiece, but taken together these biblical oratorios constitute a masterly body of work, equaled only by that of Giacomo Carissimi, the inventor of the oratorio genre a hundred years before.

Interestingly, figures from the Books of Maccabees appear in two of these fifteen oratorios—Judas Maccabeus and Alexander Balus. Although Handel came from a Lutheran area of Germany, and was composing oratorios for the Anglicans of the British Isles, neither his librettist nor his audiences seem to have had any compunction about being involved with works of music drawn from the deuterocanonical books of the Bible, which the Protestant had rejected. So, soon after the Reformation, the battle lines had not yet been drawn indicating that the Protestants would have nothing to do with those books.

Handel dedicated his Maccabean oratorios to the Duke of Cumberland, Prince William Augustus, in honor of his victorious return from the Battle of Culloden on April 16, 1746. Interestingly, the oratorios draw on Catholic books of the Bible to celebrate the defeat of the Catholic Jacobite forces. They seem to have had no awareness of this paradox, which indicates that for them, the deuterocanonical books were not identified as Roman Catholic, but were accepted as part of the common Christian heritage. In Judas Maccabeus, they could find a hero to compare with their own victorious general.

> Oh let eternal honors crown his name;
> Judas! first worthy in the rolls of fame.
> Say, "He put on the breast-plate as a giant,
> And girt his warlike harness about him;
> In his acts he was like a lion,
> And like a lion's whelp roaring for his prey."
> From mighty kings he took the spoil,
> And with his acts made Judah smile.
> Judah rejoiceth in his name,
> And triumphs in her hero's fame.
> Hail, hail, Judea, happy land!
> Salvation prospers in his hand.
>
> —Words by Thomas Morell
> for the oratorio Judas Maccabaeus by Handel

Judas Maccabeus, his brothers and countrymen went into battle when ungodly men profaned God's temple and threatened the practice of their Jewish faith. They did not go into battle for war lust or the thrill of the chase. Rather, they were fighting a "just war" for God, and to preserve their freedom to practice their religion.

1. Describe Judas Maccabeus. 1 Maccabees 3:1–10

2. Explain the sequence of events in the following verses.

1 Maccabees 3:13–15
1 Maccabees 3:16–17
1 Maccabees 3:18–22
1 Maccabees 3:23–24
1 Maccabees 3:25–26

3. How did Antiochus respond to the victory of Judas and his men?

1 Maccabees 3:27
1 Maccabees 3:28–31
1 Maccabees 3:32–36
1 Maccabees 3:37–38

4. What does the Catholic Church teach about the conditions for a "just war?"

CCC 2308 *All citizens*
CCC 2309
CCC 2309
CCC 2309 — *there must be serious prospects of* _____
CCC 2309

* Do you think that Judas was involved in a "just war?" Why or why not?

** Based on the above criteria, identify one "just war" of the past century.

5. For what cause was Judas fighting? 1 Maccabees 3:43

6. Which men did Judas excuse from fighting in the battle? 1 Maccabees 3:56

7. How did the people of God react and prepare for battle?

1 Maccabees 3:44
1 Maccabees 3:45
1 Maccabees 3:46–47
1 Maccabees 3:50–53
1 Maccabees 3:54

8. How did Judas encourage his men prior to battle? 1 Maccabees 3:58–60

9. What common theme can you find in the following verses?

1 Maccabees 3:60
Matthew 6:10
Mark 14:36

10. Whose example can help a person accept and submit to God's will? Luke 1:38

* What helps you to accept God's will in difficult circumstances?

11. How did Judas summon an army? 2 Maccabees 8:1–5

12. By what tactics did Judas fight the enemy? 2 Maccabees 8:6–8

13. How did Judas exhort and encourage his men?

2 Maccabees 8:16–17	
2 Maccabees 8:18	
2 Maccabees 8:19–21	
2 Maccabees 8:22–23	

14. What happened in the battle against Nicanor?

2 Maccabees 8:24–26	
2 Maccabees 8:27–31	
2 Maccabees 8:32–33	
2 Maccabees 8:34–36	

15. What indicates that Judas was an observant Jew? 2 Maccabees 8:26–29

16. What aim did Antiochus Epiphanes have toward the Jews? 2 Maccabees 9:1–4

* How should Catholics relate to the Jewish people? CCC 839

17. How was Antiochus punished and by whom?

2 Maccabees 9:5–7	
2 Maccabees 9:8–10	
2 Maccabees 9:11–12	

18. What last-ditch effort did Antiochus make? 2 Maccabees 9:13–19

19. Describe Antiochus' letter to the Jews. 2 Maccabees 9:19–27

20. Explain how the end of Antiochus is described. 2 Maccabees 9:28–29

* What do you expect people will say about you at the end of your life?

CHAPTER 19

Rededication of the Temple
1 Maccabees 4–6
2 Maccabees 10–11

Therefore bearing ivy-wreathed wands and beautiful branches
and also fronds of palm,
they offered hymns of thanksgiving
to him who had given success
to the purifying of his own holy place.
2 Maccabees 10:7

First Maccabees reports that Antiochus Epiphanes ordered the Jews: *to sacrifice swine and unclean animals* (1 Maccabees 1:47). Second Maccabees mentions this abomination obliquely: *The altar was covered with abominable offerings which were forbidden by the laws* (2 Maccabees 6:5). Among the animals sacrificed in Greek and Roman temples were pigs, the most unclean of all animals: *Their flesh you shall not eat, and their carcasses you shall not touch* (Deuteronomy 14:8).

After sacrifice, priests received part of the offering for their sustenance and for their families, and the remainder was given to the people. When they tried to force pork down the throat of Eleazar, and the mother with her seven sons (2 Maccabees 6:18, 7:1), the meat may already have been offered in sacrifice. Hence, they were being compelled to communicate with idolaters, in violation of the first commandment: *"You shall have no other gods before me"* (Exodus 20:3, Deuteronomy 5:7).

Each year on the festival of Ambarvalia, which took place on the twenty-fifth of May, the Romans purified their fields with three-fold sacrifice—of a white pig *sus,* a white sheep *ovis,* and a white bull *taurus.* They called this *Suovetaurilia (sus+ovis+taurus).* Cato the Elder describes the ritual and records the text of the prayers (Cato the Elder, *De Agri Cultura,* On Agriculture, 141), the oldest surviving book of Latin prose, contemporary with Maccabees, around 160 BC. Virgil gives a poetic description of the ritual in *Georgics* (Virgil, *Georgics,* 1.345). Also, this ritual is depicted on at least two major Roman monuments:

1) the column of Trajan (AD 113), in front of the Basilica Ulpia;
2) the decennial column (AD 303), in front of the Senate House.

The Greek equivalent of Suovetaurilia was the *Trittoiai* (Triple Ritual), offered to the sea god Poseidon in Homer's *Odyssey.* The sky god Zeus held the highest place in the Greek pantheon, and so the Syrians called the Jewish sanctuary—the Temple of Olympian Zeus, and they called sanctuary of the Samaritans on Mount Gerizim *the Temple of Zeus the Friend of Strangers* (2 Maccabees 6:2).

The Romans also used their ceremony of Suovetaurilia to purify the site of a temple that had been destroyed. When the Flavians captured Rome at the end of the year AD 69, the Capitoline Temple in the city was burned, and they performed such a ritual to purify the site before rebuilding. Ironically the Antiochene priests may have sacrificed swine with sheep and bulls, precisely for the purpose of dedicating the altar in Jerusalem for their worship. In the process of so doing, they desecrated and desacralized it for any Jewish worship.

The sheep and the bull were clean animals to the Jews, and could be offered in the temple, but the offering of swine was a totally shocking sacrilege. The greatest of horrors lay, however, not in what was offered but to whom it was offered. Sacrificing even a spotless lamb to Zeus or Athena would have desecrated the altar of God just as much as the sacrificing of swine. The same altar could not be used for the worship of gods both false and True. When the temple was desecrated, the land became polluted. As long as the Holy Land was unclean, the whole world was thrown out of kilter. No Jew anywhere could rest easily if false gods were worshipped and unclean sacrifices were offered before the holy place in Jerusalem.

Victory at Emmaus—Judas the Maccabee with three thousand under-equipped men (1 Maccabees 4:6) managed to defeat the five thousand foot-soldiers and one thousand horse-soldiers of the Syrian general Gorgias (1 Maccabees 4:1). What was the strategy that led to this successful outcome over larger forces?

Earlier, the three Syrian commanders—Ptolemy, Nicanor and Gorgias—divided up the forces assigned to them. Out of forty thousand foot soldiers, Gorgias got five thousand, or one-eighth of the total Syrian infantry. Out of seven thousand horse soldiers, Gorgias got one thousand, or one-seventh of the total Syrian cavalry. So, Judas selected the smallest of the three Syrian divisions to engage, and while the Syrian numbers were larger, they were not overwhelmingly so. Judas' decision seems to reflect good military horse-sense.

Judas was aided by the element of surprise. The Syrians were billetted in camp. The horses were still corralled, separated from the cavalrymen. The weapons were in the armory, separated from the infantry men. Men were resting, or having breakfast. The surprise factor more than evened the odds in favor of Judas and his forces.

After the battlefield victory, the Syrians made an inglorious retreat towards the coast, through hostile country that the Jews knew well. Three thousand Syrians fell that day, fully half the total force. There have been worse defeats in military history, like the Charge of the Light Brigade, Pickett's charge, and the Battle of the Little Big Horn. Still, three thousand was still a relatively large number of losses on a single day of battle. On the average, each Jewish soldier killed one invader.

The following year Lysias sent a second expeditionary force against the Maccabees, this time sending sixty thousand infantry—increased from forty thousand the time before.

He also sent five thousand cavalry—decreased from seven thousand the time before. This seems to indicate that the Syrians were adapting to the deployment and had learned that the cavalry were not so helpful against a guerrilla army. While Syrian numbers were impressive, the caliber of their soldiery had been dissipated by recent battlefield losses against both the Romans to the west and the Persians to the east. They had lost many of their best men, and were sending their second string forces against the Jews. They still failed to understand how serious a threat Judas posed to them, and they paid even a greater price the second time, losing five thousand this time (1 Maccabees 4:34).

Rededicating the temple on the 25th of the month—While the Syrians were licking their wounds and trying to bribe people into their armies as mercenaries, the Maccabees had secured the countryside enough to be able to re-establish proper worship in Jerusalem. *It happened that on the same day on which the sanctuary had been profaned by the foreigners, the purification of the sanctuary took place, that is, on the twenty-fifth day of the same month, which was Chislev* (2 Maccabees 10:5). The Jewish lunar month of Chislev falls at the time of the winter solstice, the shortest day of the year and the first day of winter season. The Antiochenes used a totally different, solar calendar of three hundred sixty five days with an extra day added every fourth year. Later, Julius Caesar would pattern his Julian Calendar upon the Seleucid Calendar, and he called the last month of the year December, falling at the same time as the Jewish month of Chislev.

The Syrians apparently dedicated the Jerusalem temple for their worship at the time of the winter solstice, later called the feast of Sol Invictus by the Romans. The Jews purposely rededicated the temple to their own worship on exactly the same date of the year: *They decreed by public ordinance and vote that the whole nation of the Jews should observe these days every year* (2 Maccabees 10:8). Hence, the later Jewish feast of Hannukah and the pagan festivals of the onset of winter coincide. Thus the Jewish feast acquired one last great festival, never mentioned in the Hebrew Bible but only in Maccabees.

> They were so very glad at the revival of their customs, when after a long time of intermission, they unexpectedly had regained the freedom of their worship, that they made it a law for their posterity, that they should keep a festival, on account of the restoration of their temple worship, for eight days. And from that time to this we celebrate this festival, and call it Lights. I suppose the reason was because there appeared to us this liberty beyond our hopes; and that thence was the name given to that festival.
>
> Josephus Flavius, *Antiquities of the Jews* xii.7.7

Relation between Hanukkah and Christmas—Many popular historians state that the date of Christmas has no relationship to the real date of Christ's birth. They point to the lack of evidence for the existence of a feast of Christmas before the fourth century. The most important witness, however, is found in the New Testament. Luke connects the announcement and birth of John the Baptist and of Jesus to feasts of the Jewish calendar. The Archangel Gabriel appears to Zechariah in the holy place of the temple as he fulfills his priestly duties. Only one priest entered the holy of holies, and only once each year, on Rosh Hashanah, the Jewish New Year, which occurs in late September. On that day, the ram's horn, the shofar, is blown to announce that God has spared his people for another year. That is a horn of salvation: *The Lord is my rock, and my fortress, and my deliverer, my God, my rock, in whom I take refuge, my shield, and the horn of my salvation* (Psalm 18:2b).

Later, the same archangel informed the Virgin Mary that her cousin Elizabeth had conceived a son, and was then in her sixth month (Luke 1:36). If John the Baptist was conceived near the end of September, then Jesus was conceived in late March, and born nine months later, at the end of December. So, Saint Luke dated the Annunciation in March and the Nativity in December, just as the Church calendar does. Clearly, the Church did not choose December 25th out of thin air, or to imitate a pagan feast on that date. The Church was clearly following Saint Luke.

By locating the event in December, Luke connects the birth of Jesus with the Jewish feast of Hanukkah. When he encounters the baby Jesus in the temple, Simeon declares: *for my eyes have seen your salvation which you have prepared in the presence of all peoples, a light for revelation to the Gentiles, and for glory to your people Israel* (Luke 2:30–32). The evangelist Matthew introduces the Magi, who were Gentiles following a star to the birthplace of the new King. The fourth evangelist, Saint John calls Jesus the light (John 1:5), and later quotes Jesus calling Himself *the light of the world* (John 8:12). Such terminology in the New Testament is a clear allusion to Hanukkah, the festival of lights.

Luke's Sequence of Events

September 25th of Year A (the beginning of autumn)—Archangel Gabriel appears to Zechariah, when he enters the Holy of Holies on Rosh Hashanah, the Jewish New Year, soon after the Fall Equinox. Shortly thereafter, John the Baptist is miraculously conceived, by his elderly parents, Zechariah and Elizabeth.

March 25th of Year B (the beginning of spring)—Soon after the Spring Equinox, the same Archangel Gabriel appears to Mary in Nazareth, and Jesus is miraculously conceived in the Virgin Mary by the power of the Holy Spirit.

June 24th of Year B (the beginning of summer)—At the Summer Solstice, the longest day of the year in the Julian calendar of the time, John the Baptist is born to Zechariah and Elizabeth.

December 25th of Year B (beginning of winter)—At the Winter Solstice, the shortest day of the year, Jesus is born in Bethlehem.

On three of these four dates, the Roman calendar contains solemnities—feasts of the highest rank. There is no evidence that a festival was ever celebrated on September 25th. The appearance of the Archangel Gabriel to Zechariah, near the Jewish New Year, provides the missing feast, the hinge linking the other solemnities. Since Rosh Hashanah, the Jewish New Year falls near the fall equinox, Saint Luke in effect locates all four Christian events on the two equinoxes—the two days when night and day are of equal length, in March and September, and the two solstices—the longest and shortest days of the year, in June and December. So historians are correct that Christmas fell near the start of winter, but the birth of John the Baptist fell at the beginning of summer, and the appearances of Saint Gabriel the Archangel at the start of spring and fall. The feasts of the Conception and Birth of Jesus, and the conception and birth of John the Baptist mark the beginnings of the four seasons.

Several times the books of Maccabees refer to celebrations on the twenty-fifth day of the month. The pagans desecrated the temple on such a date: *And on the twenty-fifth day of the month they offered sacrifice on the altar which was upon the altar of burnt offering* (1 Maccabees 1:59). Then the Jews rededicated the altar on the same date. At the very season and on the very day that the Gentiles had profaned it, it was re-dedicated. *It happened that on the same day on which the sanctuary had been profaned by the foreigners, the purification of the sanctuary took place, that is, on the twenty-fifth day of the same month, which was Chislev* (2 Maccabees 10:5). Early in the morning on the twenty-fifth day of the ninth month, they rose and offered sacrifice, as the law directs, on the new altar of burnt offering. The day of abomination became also the day of restoration. Since pagans and Jews calibrated feast days on corresponding days of the year, Saint Luke has good precedent for laying the groundwork for Christian feasts on the four quadrants of the solar year.

Father of Heav'n! from Thy eternal throne,
Look with an eye of blessing down,
While we prepare with holy rites,
To solemnize the feast of lights.
And thus our grateful hearts employ;
And in Thy praise
This altar raise,
with carols of triumphant joy.
See, see yon flames, that from the altar broke,
In spring streams pursue the trailing smoke.
The fragrant incense mounts the yielding air;
Sure presage that the Lord hath heard our pray'r.

—*Words by Thomas Morell*
for the oratorio Judas Maccabaeus by Handel

1. How did Judas prepare his men for battle? 1 Maccabees 4:8–11

2. What did Judas' men do after their victory? 1 Maccabees 4:24

3. Describe the main points of Judas' prayer. 1 Maccabees 4:30–33

4. What did Judas do with respect to the temple?

1 Maccabees 4:36–41
1 Maccabees 4:42–51
1 Maccabees 4:52–58
1 Maccabees 4:59–61

* What would you do if your church were desecrated and needed rededication?

5. Describe the activity in 1 Maccabees 5:1–8.

6. Who liberated the Galilean Jews? 1 Maccabees 5:9–23

7. Describe the drama in 1 Maccabees 5:24–44.

1 Maccabees 5:24–27	
1 Maccabees 5:27–34	
1 Maccabees 5:35–39	
1 Maccabees 5:40–44	

8. Identify a peaceable offering that Judas made. 1 Maccabees 5:45–49

9. Why did Joseph, Azariah, and some priests fall? 1 Maccabees 5:56–67

* Have you ever tried to make a name for yourself, but fell flat instead?

10. Describe the last days of King Antiochus Epiphanes. 1 Maccabees 6:1–31

1 Maccabees 6:1–7
1 Maccabees 6:8–13
1 Maccabees 6:14–17

11. What did Judas and Eleazar do? 1 Maccabees 6:32–47

12. What terms were offered? 1 Maccabees 6:55–63

13. How was the temple purified? 2 Maccabees 10:1–4

** How and when do you purify your temple? 1 Corinthians 3:16–17

14. When and how was the temple rededicated? 2 Maccabees 10:5–8

15. What treachery can be found in 2 Maccabees 10:14–23?

* Give some examples of the temptation of money corrupting people today.

** What could someone do to keep wealth in proper perspective?

16. What followed Judas' defeat of Timothy? 2 Maccabees 10:37–38

17. What did Lysius come to understand? 2 Maccabees 11:1–14

18. Describe the terms Maccabeus accepted. 2 Maccabees 11:15

19. Describe the following letters.

2 Maccabees 11:16–21
2 Maccabees 11:22–26
2 Maccabees 11:27–33
2 Maccabees 11:34–38

20. List ways in which Christians can witness for God and advance a godly culture.

CCC 2044
CCC 2045
CCC 2046

* What are some practical ways to preserve our Catholic culture?

CHAPTER 20

Death and Prayer
1 Maccabees 7–9
2 Maccabees 12–15

Therefore he made atonement for the dead,
that they might be delivered from their sin.
2 Maccabees 12:45

Judas the Maccabee had a string of five victories against superior Syrian forces. His army grew in size, from six hundred men at first, to twenty thousand men within five years. Syrian forces also grew, from two thousand to fifty thousand at their peak. Neither Jews nor Syrians could sustain so large an army, however; the Syrians were using mercenaries, and the Jews grew weary of annual battles. The Syrian army turned against king Antiochus Epiphanes, arrested and killed him, and enthroned Demetrius in his place. The Jewish army abandoned Judas to fight one last battle at impossible odds of twenty-two to one. His deeds stood the test of time, however, and the Jews were able to keep both their land and their religion.

Battles of Judas Maccabeus

167 BC	Judas' 600 men ambush Apollonius' 2,000 men at Nahal al-Haramia.
167 BC	Judas' 1,000 men defeat Seron's 4,000 men at Beth-Horon.
166 BC	Judas' 3,000 men defeat Gorgias' 6,000 men at Emmaus.
164 BC	Judas' 10,000 defeat Lysias' 65,000 men and 22 elephants at Beth Zur.
163 BC	Judas defeats Timotheus of Ammon's 5,000 men at Dathema.
162 BC	Lysias' 50,000 men and 30 elephants defeat Judas' 20,000 men at Beth Zechariah. Eleazar Horan, crushed by a dying elephant in battle, dies.
162 BC	Battle of Salama.
161 BC	Judas defeats Nicanor's 9,000 at Adasa and makes Adar 13 a feast day.
160 BC	Bacchides' 22,000 men defeat Judas' 1000 men at Elasa. Many of Judas' men have abandoned him and Judas now dies in battle.

Prayers for the fallen—The second part of the First Commandment (in the Catholic listing), which becomes the Second Commandment for the Protestant people, reads: *"You shall not make for yourself a graven image"* (Exodus 20:4, Deuteronomy 5:8). This commandment forbids idolatry. Based on their understanding of this law, ancient Jewish and Islamic artists avoided portraiture, and only in the Middle Ages did artists begin to depict animals and people in art and sculpture.

Judas must have recruited some inactive Jews of mixed customs. Some of the soldiers may have been of Canaanite or Greek ancestry, but sympathetic with Judas and his cause. One of these semi-Jewish battalions was recruited near the coastal city of Jamnia, and these men wore amulets (good luck charms) given by their loved ones as they left for battle. At the Battle of Dathema in 162 BC, that battalion was largely wiped out. Afterwards, all the fallen were found to be wearing these talismans (2 Maccabees 12:40). The amulets of Jamnia depicted the Canaanite gods of that city, probably the god Dagon (mentioned 1 Maccabees 11:4).

Why did Judas take up a collection of two thousand drachmas of silver and send it to Jerusalem as a sin offering? The author of Second Maccabees says: *In doing this he acted very well and honorably, taking account of the resurrection. For if he were not expecting that those who had fallen would rise again, it would have been superfluous and foolish to pray for the dead. But if he was looking to the splendid reward that is laid up for those who fall asleep in godliness, it was a holy and pious thought. Therefore he made atonement for the dead, that they might be delivered from their sin* (2 Maccabees 12:43–45).

For the second time, the doctrine of resurrection appears forcefully in the book of Second Maccabees. Earlier, the second of the seven martyred brothers declared, *"You accursed wretch, you dismiss us from this present life, but the King of the universe will raise us up to an everlasting renewal of life, because we have died for his laws"* (2 Maccabees 7:9). Their mother said to them, *"Therefore the Creator of the world, who shaped the beginning of man and devised the origin of all things, will in his mercy give life and breath back to you again, since you now forget yourselves for the sake of his laws"* (2 Maccabees 7:23).

The actions of Judas in soliciting a sin offering for the fallen must be taken in the light of those earlier professions of faith. The situation of the fallen was mixed—on the one hand, they had fought and died for the faith in the true God, but on the other, they were wearing medals of false gods. Judas confronts this theological dilemma and discovers an inspired solution. By virtue of the doctrine of the resurrection, the dead are merely asleep, awaiting the last day. So Judas makes an offering for them, as if they were in fact still living, as was done every day in the temple in Jerusalem by the living for the benefit of the living and for others.

Later, this passage becomes theologically contentious in the dispute over whether Purgatory exists. Catholic doctrine says "yes." Some traditions are mute on the subject, or contrary, and this passage in Second Maccabees provided a reason to reject the canonicity of the book. There is no corresponding passage in First Maccabees, yet that book is banned as well, a kind of guilt by association.

> *The Catechism of the Catholic Church* defines Purgatory as "a state of final purification after death and before entrance into heaven for those who died in God's friendship, but were only imperfectly purified; a final cleansing of human imperfection before one is able to enter the joy of heaven" (CCC, Glossary, p. 896).

Judas was a member of the priestly tribe of Levi, and even receives the honorary title of High Priest. His brothers Jonathan and Simon certainly claimed that title for themselves. Hence Judas acted with the authority of those who *sit on Moses' seat* (Matthew 23:2). Simon, Judas' brother, founded a line of high priests that presided at the temple for over the next century. The precedent of sin offerings for the dead, that Judas established, would certainly have been continued by his nephew John Hyrcanus I (134–104 BC), and by his great-great-nephew Hyrcanus II (75–66 BC). No evidence can be found that any high priest repudiated praying for the dead up to the very destruction of the temple by the Romans in AD 70.

Amazingly, Jesus Christ offered the perfect sacrifice of atonement for the dead on the altar of the Cross. He obtained mercy not just for the living, or for those yet to be born. His salvific action was also retroactive, and the doctrine of the descent into hell, found in the Creed affirms that Jesus rescued all the just people who were unable to enter heaven because they had died before His time. Among the men Jesus redeemed on the Cross were Adam, Noah, Abraham, Isaac, Jacob, Joseph, Moses—and Judas the Maccabee. Judas' gift of two thousand drachmas could not win salvation for his soldiers, for only Jesus could do that. Judas' goal was more modest, as the author of Second Maccabees clearly explains. He wished to offer sacrifice for their sins of idolatry, and he wanted them to awaken on the Last Day, without the image of a false god hanging around their necks.

The Alliance with Rome—The Maccabees opposed Syrian rule, thus supporting the growing power of Rome. The Syrians hated Rome; the Jews were foes of the Syrians. There is a saying, "The enemy of my enemy is my friend." Thus, for a number of years, the Jews and Romans were aligned, giving each other de facto support. For a long time Rome and Jerusalem had already shared a common cultural enemy. The historic foe of the Jews was Canaan, with false gods demanding human sacrifice, including the sacrifice of infants. The historic foe of Rome was Carthage, which had been founded by the Phoenicians. The same false gods who corrupted the Canaanites also corrupted the Carthaginians. Dagon had temples in both places. Jews and Romans reacted in genuine horror to the unspeakable rites, which took place in his temples. The Jews knew that the Romans had fought three Punic Wars in 264 BC, 218 BC and 149 BC, and destroyed the Carthaginian Empire. The author of First Maccabees alludes to this with these words: *They also subdued the kings who came against them from the ends of the earth, until they crushed them and inflicted great disaster upon them* (1 Maccabees 8:4).

Before his death, Judas sent Eupolemus and his own nephew Jason to Rome to seal this alliance by a formal treaty (1 Maccabees 8:17). This action demonstrates that Judas was a great diplomat, as well as a great general. Diplomatic and military skills do not often go together. At that time, Rome was still a republic, and the Jews were greatly impressed by their government.

After the death of Judas, his brother Jonathan sent a second delegation to Rome, to assure them of continued alliance (1 Maccabees 12:1). After the death of Jonathan, his brother Simon sent a great shield made of gold along with a third delegation headed by Numenius, to reconfirm the treaty with Rome (1 Maccabees 14:24). Each new government in Judea sent an olive branch of peace to Rome.

In AD 70 the armies of Rome would destroy Jerusalem, and soon thereafter rabbis met in Jamnia to fix the canon of the Hebrew Bible. Among their reasons for excluding First Maccabees was the rosy picture of the Romans that it presented. In fact, however, Eupolemus and Jason reported quite prophetically of the Romans to Judas the Maccabee: *but with their friends and those who rely on them they have kept friendship. They have subdued kings far and near, and as many as have heard of their fame have feared them* (1 Maccabees 8:12). Judas heeded this advice, as did all subsequent Jewish leaders for two centuries; only when the leadership finally acted to the contrary did disaster ensue.

The death of a leader—A military genius, untaught but leading the fighting, Judas the Maccabee appeared out of nowhere, as did Jesus of Nazareth, a religious genius, untaught but teaching. Both of them created a people capable of greater things—a people whose historic state had been crushed by the forces of history, a people sent into exile for many decades, a people oppressed in their own homeland. Through the career of Judas, the Jews became a regional military force to be reckoned with, after having successfully challenged one of the great powers of the day. Through the ministry of Jesus Christ, a spiritual movement began to spread out from Judea to the very ends of the earth.

In both cases, the efforts of Judas and Jesus ended in death, but the force of their personalities and their achievements made the eventual success of their movements inevitable. Death was not the end for Judas—and he really believed that! And, death was not the end for Jesus, either. Sadly, followers and disciples abandoned both Judas and Jesus. Before the battle of Elasa, the soldiers of Judas slipped away from him: *When they saw the huge number of the enemy forces, they were greatly frightened, and many slipped away from the camp, until no more than eight hundred of them were left* (1 Maccabees 9:6). At the garden of Gethsemane, the disciples of Jesus ran away in fear: *And they all deserted him and fled* (Mark 14:50).

Would the outcome have been different, if the followers had stayed with Judas and Jesus? Judas loved his soldiers and did not wish them harm, even as they were abandoning him to his fate. Jesus loved His disciples, and was willing to die for them. Still, to be left alone by so many loved ones must have been a cruel blow to the hearts of them both. In the Stations of the Cross, the modern followers of Jesus recall the stages of His Passion. Someone, whether Jewish or Christian, should also remember the passion of Judas the Maccabee.

The fruits of the Maccabees—Jews do not have Maccabees in their Bible, but they know about those writings. Though the Maccabees are in the Catholic canon (two books) and Eastern canon (four books), the biblically literate Christian is barely conscious of them. Yet, as Jesus said, *"You will know them by their fruits"* (Matthew 7:16). So what fruits did the Maccabees produce? Above all, they were a family of leaders, courageously committed to defending their faith and the practice of their religion at all costs. In two generations they produced four commanders for the armies and people of Judea.

The Five Sons of Mattathias †166 BC

†162 BC — Eleazar Avaran died killing an elephant at Beth Zechariah.
†160 BC — John Gaddi died at the battle of Elasa in 160 BC.
†160 BC — Judas Maccabeus was general from 166–160 BC.
He died with his brother in the battle at Elasa in 160 BC.
†142 BC — Jonathan Apphus was a military general from 160–142 BC.
He was co-governor and high priest from 152–142 BC.
†135 BC — Simon Thassi was governor from 166–135 BC.
He was the high priest from 142–135 BC.

Simon and Judas shared the mandate after the death of their father. Simon and Jonathan co-ruled after the death of their brother Judas. Simon ruled alone after the death of Jonathan. So, the unsung hero of the Maccabean revolt was Simon. He shared the command of the nation for thirty years, from the death of his father in 166 BC to his own death in 135 BC. Judas was a public face for the revolt, but Simon was the quiet one, organizing behind the scenes. Occasionally, he did lead part of the army into battle, and he distinguished himself with important military victories. His principal contribution, though, was the management of the civil affairs of the nation. He was a part-time general, but a full-time governor. For the last ten years of his life, Simon was also the high priest. The ability of these brothers to share responsibilities without conflict among themselves was a principal factor contributing to their success.

Psalm 133

Behold, how good and pleasant it is
when brothers dwell in unity!
It is like the precious oil upon the head,
running down upon the beard,
upon the beard of Aaron,
running down on the collar of his robes!
It is like the dew of Hermon,
which falls upon the mountains of Zion!
For there the Lord has commanded the blessing,
life for evermore.

---

1. Write one sentence to describe the following sections of 1 Maccabees 7.

1 Maccabees 7:1–11	
1 Maccabees 7:12–25	
1 Maccabees 7:26–32	
1 Maccabees 7:33–38	
1 Maccabees 7:39–50	

2. Why might an alliance with Rome be desirable? 1 Maccabees 8:1–16

3. Explain the alliance between the Maccabees and Romans. 1 Maccabees 8:17–32

4. What treachery occurred and how did Judas respond?

1 Maccabees 9:5–7	
1 Maccabees 9:8–10	

* Recall a time in your life when you felt deserted or abandoned by your friends.

5. Describe the last battle of Judas. 1 Maccabees 9:11–18

6. Who buried Judas and how was he mourned? 1 Maccabees 9:19–22

7. What followed the death of Judas? 1 Maccabees 9:23–36

8. How did John's brothers avenge his death? 1 Maccabees 9:37–42

9. How and why did Jonathan begin to fight Bacchides? 1 Maccabees 9:43–49

10. What happened when Alcimus desecrated the sanctuary? 1 Maccabees 9:54–57

11. How did Jonathan bring the war to an end? 1 Maccabees 9:58–73

* Describe a peacemaker you know, or a time that *you* were a peacemaker.

12. In one sentence each, describe each of the following military campaigns.

2 Maccabees 12:1–9
2 Maccabees 12:10–16
2 Maccabees 12:17–25
2 Maccabees 12:26–31
2 Maccabees 12:32–38

13. What did Judas find when he went to bury the dead? 2 Maccabees 12:39–40

14. How does the Church see lucky charms and magic? CCC 2111, 2116–2117

* What contemporary ways do people use to disobey the first Commandment?

15. What specific things did Judas do for the dead, and why?

2 Maccabees 12:41–42
2 Maccabees 12:43
2 Maccabees 12:44–45

16. What kindness can we show to for our deceased loved ones? CCC 1371

** What do you usually offer at the death of a relative or friend? Why?

17. Use the Bible and Catechism to explain Purgatory.

1 Corinthians 3:15
1 Peter 1:7
CCC 1030
CCC 1031
CCC 1032

18. Summarize the main events in 2 Maccabees 13:1–26.

19. Contrast Alcimus' and Nicanor's impressions of Judas. 2 Maccabees 14:1–46

20. In whom did Judas put all his trust and confidence? 2 Maccabees 15:7–34

* What and in whom do people put their faith in today? What about you?

CHAPTER 21

Priestly Rule
1 Maccabees 10–16

So Jonathan put on the holy garments
in the seventh month of the one hundred and sixtieth year,
at the feast of tabernacles,
and he recruited troops and equipped them with arms in abundance.
1 Maccabees 10:21

When their rebellion began, the Maccabees probably did not give very much thought to the kind of state they wanted to create. They knew what they did not want however, which was what they had. They could not reach back into recent history for a paradigm of governance, nor could the monarchy of old serve as a model for them, because they were not of the tribe of Judah, or of the lineage of David. Hence they could not restore the kingdom.

At the end of chapter nine, First Maccabees hearkens back to the time of the Judges, as he describes the peacetime activities of Jonathan: *Thus the sword ceased from Israel. And Jonathan dwelt in Michmash. And Jonathan began to judge the people, and he destroyed the ungodly out of Israel* (1 Maccabees 9:73). In nearly every way, however, the Maccabees differed from the judges of old. The judges claimed anointing by God to rule only in times of war, and they never set up any dynasty. The Maccabees had no anointing, other than their own faith and zeal, but they ruled in times of peace, as well as in times of war. And, the Maccabees did set up a dynasty that ruled for over a century.

The Reign of Jonathan—Five years after the revolt in 166 BC, Jonathan claimed the high priesthood, thus combining clerical and lay duties in his person (1 Maccabees 10:21). Now, the proper functions of the priestly tribe of Levi are to bless the people, conduct ritual sacrifices, and sing praise in the temple. The only members of this tribe who ever ruled were Moses and at least one of the judges. The collapse of other organs of national life left only the priesthood functional, and the Maccabees stepped into the void. The problem with clerical rule is that lay people become excluded from their proper role in the state. In the case of Israel, the right to rule belonged only to the lineage of David, of the tribe of Judah, and the Maccabees instead were Levites. By taking upon themselves governmental and military duties as well as priestly ones, the Maccabees set up their descendants for role conflicts.

The chief challenge that Jonathan faced in his twenty-year reign (161–142 BC) was the invasion by the Egyptian ruler Ptolemy VI Philometer in 145 BC. The Egyptians managed to take the entire kingdom of Syria, but the victorious Ptolemy died of wounds suffered in battle, only three days after the beheading of his vanquished son-in-law

Alexander Balus. Jonathan had to retake Jerusalem by military strategy and diplomacy: *Then Jonathan asked the king to free Judea and the three districts of Samaria from tribute, and promised him three hundred talents* (1 Maccabees 11:28).

> Mysterious are thy ways, O Providence!
> But always true and just. By Thee kings reign,
> By Thee they fall. —Where is now Egypt's boast?
> Where thine, O Syria, laid low in dust,
> While chosen Judah triumphs in success,
> And feels the presence of Jehovah's arm.
> Mindful of this, let Israel ever fear,
> With filial reverence, his tremendous name,
> And with obsequious hearts exalt his praise.
> Ye servants of th' eternal King,
> His pow'r and glory sing,
> And speak of all his righteous ways
> With wonder and with praise.
> Amen. Hallelujah. Amen.
>
> —*Words by Thomas Morell*
> *for the oratorio Alexander Balus by Handel*

The Reign of Simon—When Jonathan died in 142 BC, his brother Simon, who had shared civil rule with his two brothers, took upon himself both the military and priestly authority. Simon was actually the elder brother, and came out of seeming retirement to head the state alone in his old age. He had served in an occasional military capacity before, but his primary task had been civilian administration. No better person could have stepped forward at this juncture to help build the institutions of the national life.

The chief challenge that Simon had to face at the very beginning of his seven years of solitary reign (142–135 BC) was the invasion by the Syrian king Demetrius in 140 BC (1 Maccabees 13). After that, he was able to complete his reign in peace: *The land had rest all the days of Simon. He sought the good of his nation; his rule was pleasing to them, as was the honor shown him, all his days* (1 Maccabees 14:4).

The Reign of John Hyrcanus I—In 135 BC, Simon Maccabee died after ruling for thirty years together with his brothers Judah and Jonathan. Subsequently, power transferred to his son John Hyrcanus for the next thirty years (134–104 BC). The First Book of Maccabees introduces the figure of John Hyrcanus, but closes before the new reign actually gets underway. Josephus, however, tells the rest of the story. Not finding enough Jews to fill the ranks of his army, John Hyrcanus had to raise a mercenary army. Thirty years before, the Syrians had hired mercenaries to try to hold the Holy Land, and now the Jews were hiring mercenaries themselves. The Hasmonean dynasty had come to look less like a popular uprising, and more like an occupying force. Commanding gentile troops was not actually part of the job description of a Jewish high priest!

With these multi-national troops, John Hyrcanus fought a spectrum of wars, destroying the Samaritan temple on Mount Gerizim in about 110 BC. The movement that fifty years before had sought freedom for Jews, now devolved into an attack on the freedom of others. Hostility between Samaritans and Jews continued into New Testament times.

John Hyrcanus ordered all the Galileans and Idumeans to convert to Judaism or be killed. Once before, the Syrians had ordered all of the Jews to convert or die, and now the Jews enforced the same policy on others. The tense relationship, between the Galileans and Judeans, in the four Gospels demonstrates this sad legacy. Many Galileans, like Saint Joseph had family origins in the south, and had to practice heroic virtue to travel through Samaritan country to attend the feasts in Jerusalem. Once there, however, their northern accent left them subject to prejudice, the imputation of being second-class Jews, pressured into the religion by force.

The narrative of the First Book of Maccabees cuts short right before these policies of John Hyrcanus were enacted, because they were not in the great tradition of Levitical priesthood or of the Davidic state. Neither Moses nor David had ever hired foreign mercenaries or destroyed temples or forced people to convert at the point of a sword. But, the Seleucid Syrians had done these things, and eventually the Hasmoneans did them too.

The Hasmonean Dynasty collapsed when they turned to Parthia for support against Rome in 41 BC. The Roman Senate named Herod, governor of Galilee, as "King of the Jews." To seal his claim, Herod married Mariamne, niece of the last Hasmonean king, but had her executed after twelve years of marriage in 29 BC. Herod also executed their two sons Alexander and Aristobolus in 7 BC. After this outrage, Herod had no compunction about killing all the baby boys of Bethlehem in his attempt to prevent the family of David from producing a true heir to his throne. The martyrdom of the Holy Innocents in Matthew is entirely consonant with the well-documented psychotic and paranoid leadership style of Herod.

The gap between the Testaments—The end of the period of God's Revelation for the Hebrew Bible occurs at Nehemiah's death in 400 BC, after which there would be no more inspired writers in Jewish canon, but only a process of editing the revealed texts. After the fall of Jerusalem in AD 70, a school of rabbinical studies at Jamnia in the Holy Land made the decisions, which led to the official list of thirty-seven books in the Hebrew Bible. The Jews gave pride of place to documents that existed in the Hebrew language, but they excluded some beautiful Hebrew texts like First Maccabees and Sirach. However, they did choose to include several Aramaic chapters within the books of Daniel, Ezra and Nehemiah. They had a vested interest in pushing the end of Revelation as far back as possible, to exclude the writings of the New Testament from any consideration.

The Christian Bible ends with the Book of Revelation, five hundred years after the death of Nehemiah. Thus, for Christians, God's self-revelation continued for half a millennium longer than for the Jews. Since Revelation lasted longer for Christians, the process of determining the canonicity of books took correspondingly longer, too. The bishops, successors of the apostles, bore the responsibility for defining canonicity of the Christian Bible. They gave pride of place to sources quoted in the New Testament, but they included the book of Nahum, which is ignored by Christian authors, along with other deuterocanonical works.

Bishops at the Council of Hippo in North Africa compiled a list of forty-six Old Testament books and twenty-seven New Testament books in AD 393, which remains the exact same list as the canon of Roman Catholic Bibles today. The councils of Carthage in 397 and 419 compiled the same list of books. In AD 1441, an ecumenical Council at Florence reaffirmed this same canon. Finally, the infallible definition of the canonical books of Sacred Scripture came from the Council of Trent in AD 1556, and the list of seventy-three books remains to this day.

After the Reformation, some Protestants began to limit the Old Testament to those books which were also accepted by the Jews. One of the principal considerations was enabling Bible publishers to print a more compact volume. Inadvertently, this strategy created a lengthy gap between the end of the Old Testament, and the beginning of the New Testament. From the death of Nehemiah to the appearance of the Archangel Gabriel at the beginning of Luke's Gospel rests a period of four hundred years. Why would the Holy Spirit choose to remain silent during those last centuries leading up to the birth of the Messiah? Of all the people who lived before Christ's coming, those people needed the ongoing gifts of the Word most.

The longer canon of the Old Testament, with the seven extra books, closes that gap between the Testaments. From the death of John Hyrcanus in 104 BC at the end of First Maccabees, to the appearance of the Archangel Gabriel in about 6 BC at the beginning of the Gospel according to Luke, there exists only a ninety-eight year gap between the two Testaments. That shortens the intertestamental period by three quarters, or three hundred years. Those who yearned for the Messiah when He came were the spiritual heirs of the Maccabees. The time was short enough to be bridged by the memory of participants in both sets of events. Some of those New Testament figures old enough to remember Hasmonean rule would include:

> ➢ Zechariah (Luke 1:5)
> ➢ Elizabeth (Luke 1:5)
> ➢ Joseph (Luke 1:27)
> ➢ Simeon (Luke 2:25)
> ➢ Anna (Luke 2:36)

The economy of salvation required something to fill the gap, but even more, to build a bridge for continuity between the Testaments. To the casual reader, there seems to be a great distance between Old and New, like the abyss in the parable of Lazarus and Dives: *"And besides all this, between us and you a great chasm has been fixed, in order that those who would pass from here to you may not be able, and none may cross from there to us"* (Luke 16:26). The deuterocanonical writings in general, and Maccabees and Sirach in particular, display how one Testament segues into the next. These books manage to be intensely Jewish—for they are written in Hebrew and profess total adherence to the precepts of the Torah of Moses. At the same time, however, they contain doctrines like the golden rule (Sirach 31:15), and the resurrection (2 Maccabees 12:43), which everyone associates with the Gospel. Without these writings, the human authors of the two Testaments could be seen as belonging to two, completely different religions.

Theologians have expended a great deal of effort comparing the Testaments. The evidence of the deuterocanonical writing shows that God intended the entirety of Revelation to be a seamless garment. There is growth from beginning to end of Revelation, but there is also growth within the Old Testament, even between Exodus and Deuteronomy, as well as in the New Testament. A superficial reading of Saint Paul could give the impression that he makes a great contrast between Law and Gospel. Actually, those two words never appear in opposition in Pauline writings, or anywhere else in the New Testament.

Maccabees function like a hinge between the Testaments. Reading these books, Christians can learn how seriously the Jewish people took their religious values in the years leading up to Christ. They were willing to fight and to give their lives for their beliefs. The Maccabees were faithful to God and courageous. And, the Jews deeply felt the need to have a king. By reading these books, Jews can learn how the ideas of saving sacrifice and of resurrection arose from their own heritage, before becoming encapsulated in the Gospel. Maccabees and other such writings constitute a door that swings both ways, giving Jews admittance to the New Testament, and providing Christians admittance to an understanding of the Old Testament.

Glimmers of Hope During the Exile

The God of the Bible is not indifferent in the face of evil. Even if his ways are not our ways, and his times and plans are different from ours (cf. Isaiah 55:8–9), yet he takes sides with the victims and will be a severe judge of the violent, the oppressor, those who triumph without showing mercy. His intervention does not seek destruction. . . .

The dream of the return of those sent into exile . . . is for the rebirth of the entire Israel, as in the happy days of the occupation of the whole of the Promised Land . . . In the Bible, the lament of those who suffer never ends in desperation, but is always open to hope. It is based on the certainty that the Lord does not abandon his children; he does not let those he made fall out of his hands.

Blessed John Paul II, *General Audience*, January 23, 2002.

1. What did Alexander and Demetrius offer to Jonathan?

1 Maccabees 10:1–5, 21–45
1 Maccabees 10:15–20

2. How did Jonathan and the Jews respond to Demetrius' words?

1 Maccabees 10:7–9
1 Maccabees 10:10–14
1 Maccabees 10:46–47

* Recall a time when you heard flowery words that you suspected were insincere.

3. Explain the treaty between Ptolemy and Alexander. 1 Maccabees 10:51–66

4. How did Jonathan and Simon face an ambush attempt? 1 Maccabees 10:74–89

5. What happened to Ptolemy and his son-in-law Alexander? 1 Maccabees 1:1–19

6. In one sentence, summarize the main events in these passages.

1 Maccabees 11:20–37	
1 Maccabees 11:38–59	
1 Maccabees 11:60–66	
1 Maccabees 11:70–74	

* Were Jonathan's troops faithful or fickle? When are you tempted to be fickle?

7. Explain the alliances that Jonathan sought. What help did he have in war?

1 Maccabees 12:1, 3–4	
1 Maccabees 12:2, 23	
1 Maccabees 12:14–15	

** Who has been a good support or alliance in your life?

8. Explain one wise defensive measure and one foolish thing Jonathan did.

1 Maccabees 12:35–38
1 Maccabees 12:39–53

9. What wisdom can you learn from the above situation? Sirach 6:7; 12:10

10. Explain some major things that Simon did.

1 Maccabees 13:1–6
1 Maccabees 13:7–11
1 Maccabees 13:12–19
1 Maccabees 13:25–30
1 Maccabees 13:41–48
1 Maccabees 13:49–53

* What are some of the wisest things you have done in your life, thus far?

11. What virtue did Simon instill in his people? *How can you grow in this virtue?

2 Maccabees 2:18
Romans 5:4–5
CCC 1817–1821

12. Describe some things about Simon from the passages below.

1 Maccabees 14:4
1 Maccabees 14:8–14
1 Maccabees 14:15
1 Maccabees 14:31–34
1 Maccabees 14:41–49

13. What godly virtue did the people find in Simon? What type of person was he?

Proverbs 3:3
1 Maccabees 14:35
CCC 897

* Describe a person who exemplifies the virtue of faithfulness.

14. What did Antiochus, son of Demetrius promise? 1 Maccabees 15:1–14

15. How did Rome relate to Simon and the Jews? 1 Maccabees 15:15–24

16. Describe the change in Antiochus' behavior. 1 Maccabees 15:25–31

17. How did Simon react to Antiochus' demands? 1 Maccabees 15:36

18. Why did Simon pass the baton to his sons? 1 Maccabees 16:1–3

19. What sin precipitated the deaths of Simon and his sons?

1 Maccabees 16:16–17
1 Corinthians 6:10
CCC 1852

20. What virtue can be developed to come against this sin?

Sirach 18:30; 37:27
CCC 1809

Come and See
Catholic Bible Study

Study the entire Catholic Bible — in 12 volumes! —

- In depth Scripture study with a profound Catholic vision
- Uses the Revised Standard Version Catholic Edition Bible (RSVCE)
- References the Catechism of the Catholic Church (CCC)
- Examines writings of early Church Fathers, and recent popes
- Commentaries by world-renowned Catholic biblical scholars
- Suitable for a large parish Bible Study or for a small home group
- Children's Bible Study books for pre-school children

About our Authors

Bishop Jan Liesen, S.S.D.—studied Sacred Scripture at the Pontifical Biblical Institute in Rome (The Biblicum), where he wrote his dissertation on the book of Sirach. He is a member of the Papal Theological Commission and the Bishop of Breda in the Netherlands. Bishop Liesen is the primary author of *Wisdom,* and *The Gospel of Mark.*

Father Joseph Ponessa, S.S.D.—studied under Cardinal Albert Vanhoye, S.J. at the The Biblicum, earning a doctorate in Sacred Scripture. He is the primary author of *The Gospel of John, Genesis, Moses and the Torah, Acts and Letters, David and the Psalms, Prophets and Apostles, Exile and Return.*

Father Ponessa, Bishop Liesen, Monsignor Kosanke

Monsignor Charles Kosanke, S.S.D.—studied Scripture at the Gregorian University in Rome. He taught Scripture at Sacred Heart Seminary and was the rector of Saints Cyril and Methodius Seminary in Michigan. Monsignor Kosanke is the primary author of *Isaiah.*

Monsignor Jan Majernik, S.S.D.—a native of Slovakia, earned a doctorate in Sacred Scripture from the Franciscan School of Biblical Studies in Jerusalem. He studied biblical archeology and biblical languages at the Hebrew University in Israel and at the Biblicum in Rome. He is the primary author of *The Synoptics.*

Father Andreas Hoeck, S.S.D.—born in Cologne, Germany, earned his doctorate at the Pontifical Biblical Institute in Rome, where he wrote his dissertation on the book of Revelation. He is the academic dean at Saint John Vianney Seminary in Denver and author of *Ezekiel, Hebrews, Revelation.*

Laurie Watson Manhardt, Ph.D.—earned a doctorate in education from the University of Michigan. She writes all of the home study questions, and the children's books. Laurie wrote the commentaries on *Leviticus, Numbers, Psalms, Proverbs, Ecclesiastes, Wisdom, Judith, Esther, Romans, Philippians, Galatians, 1 and 2 Timothy, Titus,* and *1 and 2 Peter.*

..................Basic, Foundational Books..................

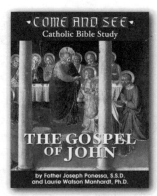

The Gospel of John
This natural starting place for Bible Study covers the life of Jesus and the institution of the sacraments of Baptism, Reconciliation, Eucharist, Holy Orders, and Matrimony.

202 pages, paperback, Item #926...$19.95 DVD, Item #954...$49.95

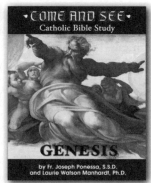

Genesis
The first book of the Bible covers the lives of Adam and Eve, Noah, Abraham, Isaac, Jacob, Esau, Joseph and his brothers. Father Ponessa looks at creation through the lens of science in this 22 chapter study.

216 pages, paperback, Item #819...$19.95 DVD, Item #994...$49.95

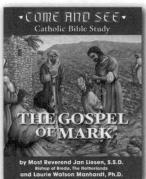

The Gospel of Mark
Bishop Liesen provides an 18 week study of the first Gospel written.

220 pages, paperback, Item #867...$19.95 DVD, Item #835...$79.95

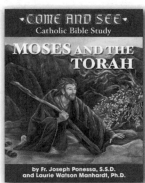

Moses and the Torah
Complete your study of the Pentateuch with *Exodus, Leviticus, Numbers,* and *Deuteronomy.*

220 pages, paperback, Item #807...$19.95 DVD, Item #808...$69.95

The Synoptics
Compare *Matthew, Mark,* and *Luke's* accounts of the life of Jesus as you journey through the Holy Land in this 22 week study.

204 pages, paperback, Item #945...$19.95 DVD, Item #947...$69.95

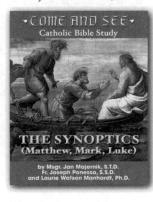

Acts and Letters
Study the early Church from the *Acts of the Apostles* and letters of Saint Paul in this 22 week study.

220 pages, paperback, Item #814...$19.95 DVD, Item #815...$69.95

Prophets and Apostles
Discover how the prophets looked forward to God's promised Messiah while the apostles see the fulfillment of those prophecies in the life of Jesus.

206 pages. paperback, Item #928...$19.95 DVD, Item #998...$49.95

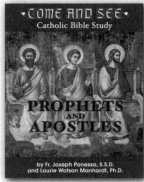

.... Advanced, Challenging Books ....

David and the Psalms
In this 22 week study, examine the lives of Ruth, Samuel, and David, and the psalms and canticles associated with them. These prayers emerge in the life of Christ and His Church.

208 pages, paperback, Item #983...$19.95
DVD, Item #996...$69.95

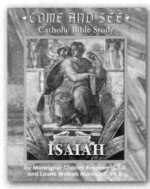

Isaiah
This major Old Testament prophet's writings have been called the fifth Gospel because his prophecies point to Jesus of Nazareth, the Suffering Servant and Redeemer of the world. This is a 22 chapter study.

214 pages, paperback, Item #855...$19.54
DVD, Item #856...$69.95

Wisdom
In this 22 chapter study, Bishop Liesen provides commentary on the Wisdom literature of the Bible: *Job, Proverbs, Ecclesiastes, Song of Solomon, Wisdom,* and *Sirach.*

220 pages, Softcover Book, Item #820...$19.95
DVD, Item #821...$69.95

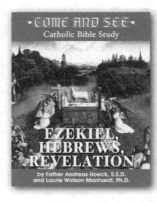

Ezekiel, Hebrews, Revelation
The prophet Ezekiel has some visions similar to those encountered by Saint John on the Island of Patmos and revealed in the *Book of Revelation. The Letter to the Hebrews* reveals Jesus the High Priest in this 22 lesson study.

220 pages, paperback, Item #834...$19.95
DVD, Item #835...$69.95

Return from Exile
In this 22 week study, *Tobit, Judith, Esther, Ezra, Nehemiah,* and *1 and 2 Maccabees* tell us about the ways in which God worked in the lives of the Jewish people as they returned from their exile in Babylon.

220 pages, paperback, $19.95
DVD

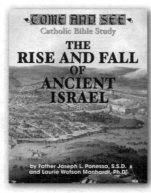

The Rise and Fall of Ancient Israel
Complete the "Come and See ~ Catholic Bible Study" series, covering all 73 books of the Catholic canon, with this study of *Joshua, Judges, 1 and 2 Kings, 1 and 2 Chronicles, Amos, Hosea,* and *Jeremiah.*

220 pages, paperback, $19.95

Come and See ~ Catholic Bible Study
www.CatholicBibleStudy.net
(772) 321-4034

Emmaus Road Publishing
827 North Fourth Street
Steubenville, OH 43952

www.EmmausRoad.org   (800) 398–5470   (740) 283-2880